CLEANSING
THE DOORS OF PERCEPTION

If the doors of perception were cleansed, everything
would appear to man as it is, infinite.

—William Blake

CLEANSING
the DOORS *of*
PERCEPTION

The Religious Significance of
Entheogenic Plants and Chemicals

HUSTON SMITH

SENTIENT PUBLICATIONS, LLC

Library of Congress Cataloging-in-Publication Data

Smith, Huston.
    Cleansing the doors of perception : the religious significance of entheogenic
plants and chemicals / Huston Smith.
       p. cm.
    Originally published: New York : J.P. Tarcher/Putnam, c2000.
    Includes bibliographical references and index.
    ISBN 1-59181-008-6
    1. Hallucinogenic drugs and religious experience. I. Title.

BL65.D7S55 2003
291.4'2—dc21   2002042946

SENTIENT PUBLICATIONS
A Limited Liability Company
1113 Spruce Street
Boulder, CO 80302
www.sentientpublications.com

To the memory of
Walter Pahnke,
and to his wife, Eva,
and their children, Kristin, David, and Jonathan

The mescaline experience is without any question the most extraordinary and significant experience available to human beings this side of the Beatific Vision. To be shaken out of the ruts of ordinary perception, to be shown for a few timeless hours the outer and inner worlds, not as they appear to an animal obsessed with survival or to a human being obsessed with words and notions, but as they are apprehended, directly and unconditionally, by Mind at Large – this is an experience of inestimable value to anyone.

—ALDOUS HUXLEY

The spiritual crisis pervading all spheres of Western industrial society can be remedied only by a change in our world view. We shall have to shift from the materialistic, dualistic belief that people and their environment are separate, toward a new consciousness of an all-encompassing reality which embraces the experiencing ego, a reality in which people feel their oneness with animate nature and all of creation.

Everything that can contribute to such a fundamental alteration in our perception of reality must therefore command earnest attention. Foremost among such approaches are the various methods of meditation, which aim to deepen the consciousness of reality by way of a total mystical experience. Another important, but still controversial, path to the same goal is the use of the consciousness-altering properties of psychopharmaceuticals.

—ALBERT HOFMANN

Ecstasy! In common parlance ecstasy is fun. But ecstasy is not fun. Your very soul is seized and shaken until it tingles. After all, who will choose to feel undiluted awe? The unknowing vulgar abuse the word; we must recapture its full and terrifying sense.

—R. GORDON WASSON

Our normal waking consciousness . . . is but one special type of consciousness, whilst all about it, parted from it by the filmiest of screens, there lie potential forms of consciousness entirely different. We may go through life without suspecting their existence; but apply the requisite stimulus, and at a touch they are there in all their completeness. . . . No account of the universe in its totality can be final which leaves these other forms of consciousness quite disregarded. How to regard them is the question,—for they are so discontinuous with ordinary consciousness. Yet they may determine attitudes though they cannot furnish formulas, and open a region though they fail to give a map. At any rate, they forbid a premature closing of our accounts with reality. Looking back on my own experiences [with nitrous oxide] they all converge toward a kind of insight to which I cannot help ascribing some metaphysical significance.

—WILLIAM JAMES

The greatest of blessings come to us through madness, when it is sent as a gift of the gods. Heaven-sent madness is superior to man-made sanity.

—PLATO, IN THE *PHAEDRUS*

CONTENTS

Preface   XV

Introduction   I

CHAPTER ONE.   Empirical Metaphysics   9

CHAPTER TWO.   Do Drugs Have Religious Import?   15

CHAPTER THREE.   Psychedelic Theophanies and the
                    Religious Life   33

CHAPTER FOUR.   Historical Evidence: India's Sacred
                    Soma   45

CHAPTER FIVE.   The Sacred Unconscious   65

CHAPTER SIX.   Contemporary Evidence: Psychiatry
                    and the Work of Stanislav Grof   79

CHAPTER SEVEN.   The Good Friday Experiment   99

CHAPTER EIGHT.   The Case of Cardinal John Henry
                    Newman   107

CHAPTER NINE.   Entheogenic Religions: The Eleusinian
                    Mysteries and the Native American
                    Church   113

CHAPTER TEN.   Something Like a Summing-Up   127

                    APPENDICES

APPENDIX A.   Secularization and the Sacred:
                    The Contemporary Scene   135

APPENDIX B.   Thinking Allowed with Jeffrey
                    Mishlove: A Televised Interview   149

Notes and References   159

Index   165

ACKNOWLEDGMENTS

I am indebted to the Council on Spiritual Practices (www.csp.org) for asking me to gather into a single volume the essays I have written on the entheogens. Without this request it would not have occurred to me to do that.

The Council has supported the project from beginning to end, and has my sincerest thanks.

PREFACE

Is it possible today, in the climate of fear created by the war on drugs, to write a book on the entheogens with the informed objectivity of Aldous Huxley's *The Doors of Perception*, the understanding that Albert Hofmann accorded the topic in *LSD: My Problem Child*, the expertise Gordon Wasson brought to it in his *SOMA*, and the open-mindedness with which William James approached the subject in *The Varieties of Religious Experience?* And is the reading public ready for such a book?

I do not know the answers to those questions, but I find myself wanting to put them to the test. My reasons are theoretical rather than adversarial, for I am more philosopher than activist. It is true that, though this book is being published as a free-standing volume in its own right, it is also listed as number five in a series of books on the entheogens – virtually nonaddictive drugs that seem to harbor spiritual potentials – that the Council on Spiritual Practices is issuing. I am comfortable with this, for not only did that Council instigate this book by asking me to pull its essays together; I support its objectives, which include working cautiously toward carving out a space where serious students of the entheogens can pursue their interests carefully and lawfully. I was fortunate in being able to do that under the umbrella of Harvard University's 1960–63 research program before it careened off-course, and it is only fair to do what I can to accord others the same opportunity.

This said, however, I come back to my concerns here being philosophical rather than programmatic. During the semester that Aldous Huxley was at M.I.T., he remarked in the course of a seminar that nothing was more curious, and to his way of thinking more important, than the role that mind-altering plants and chemicals have played in human history. Add to that William James's point that no account of the universe in its totality can be taken as final if it ignores extraordinary experiences of the sort he himself encountered through the use of nitrous oxide. This entire book can be seen as an extended meditation on those two ideas.

As for the other two parties that I mentioned in my opening paragraph (and who join Huxley and James on the frontispiece of this book), I will defer until chapter 4 the story of the summer I spent working with Gordon Wasson on his claim that India's sacramental plant, soma, was a psychoactive mushroom. Albert Hofmann, the discoverer of LSD, I include not only for the judiciousness of his discussion of his problem child, but for a personal reason as well. A friend of mine who visited him in Switzerland had occasion to mention my book *Forgotten Truth,* which outlines the metaphysical position – roughly the Great Chain of Being – that my entheogenic encounters enabled me to experience. When my friend returned from that visit and told me that Hofmann had expressed interest in my book, I sent him a copy. The letter I received in reply opened by saying, "No other book in the last years has meant more to me than your *Forgotten Truth.* My experience and awareness of reality and its different aspects correspond completely with your view. The reward I got by studying your book was to find my insights, which are those of a natural scientist, a layman in philosophy, confirmed and expanded more fully by a professional in this field."

The essays in this book span almost forty years. I have edited them liberally, excising repetitions and passages I no longer consider important. Each essay is introduced by a statement that notes the occasion for which it was written and locates it on the trajectory of the book as a whole. My intent has been to produce a work that touches on the major facets of its enigmatic subject as seen through the eyes of someone (myself) who, given my age, may have thought and written more about it than anyone else alive.

Nomenclature has been a problem. I never use the word "hallucinogen" because error is built into its definition – *Webster's New Universal Unabridged Dictionary* defines "hallucination" as "(1) the apparent perception of sights, sounds, etc., that are not actually present [which] may occur in certain mental disorders; (2) the imaginary object apparently seen, heard, etc." The word "psychedelic" is etymologically innocuous, literally meaning "mind-manifesting," but it is dated, tagged to "the psychedelic sixties" when recreational use of drugs took over, and thus clearly inappropriate when speaking of shamans, Eleusis, and the Native American Church. We need a word that designates virtually nonaddictive mind-altering substances that are approached seriously and reverently, and the word "entheogens" does just that. It is not without problems of its own, for etymologically it suggests "God-containing," whereas "God-enabling" would be more accurate – Aldous Huxley told me never to say that chemicals *cause* visionary experiences; say that they *occasion* them. I retain "psychedelic" in the early essays of this book which were written when it was the going word, but, thereafter, I follow the lead of Wasson, Hofmann, Richard Schultes, and other pioneers in concluding that "entheogens" is the appropriate word for mind-changing substances when they are taken sacramentally.

HUSTON SMITH
Berkeley, California

INTRODUCTION

This book opens with a description of my first entheogen experience, and – because objective understanding of these substances is the book's primary aim – this leaves me with no alternative but to talk about myself; for there is no direct line from chemical brain states to the experiences they occasion. Invariably the psychological makeup of the subject (his "set," as investigators call it) acts as a filter, as do the circumstances surrounding the ingestion, its "setting." The reader needs to be aware of this, for whether I am reporting experiences I have had or registering conclusions that I have reached on the tricky issues this book takes up, I (the book's author) am inevitably present in its pages for establishing the angle from which the subject is viewed. The object of this Introduction is to make that angle clear, and it can be relatively brief, for only things that bear on the book's subject need be included.

Set

As far back as I can remember, my recollections have a metaphysical tinge to them and bodings of ultimacy. My parents were Protestant missionaries in rural China, and as disease was rampant it is not surprising that my earliest memory is of a burning fever during which I was rationed to a teaspoonful of boiled water every forty-five minutes because that was as much as my stomach could keep down. Those intolerably long waits, the desperate thirst! *Dukkha,* life is suffering, the first of the Buddha's Four Noble Truths. In a second illness (a year or so later) my fever reached the proportions of delirium, and I experienced my body as distended and filling the bedroom like a balloon. Metaphysics stalks such memories, for suffering raises the question of why it occurs, and delirium (by showing that the world can appear in radically different guises) raises the question of which guise is real. Did Chuang Tzu dream that he was a butterfly, or was his "waking" state a butterfly's dream?

When thoughts begin to enter my memories, they too have metaphysical edges. Whether the memory is of waking on a wintry night to the unbelievable splendor of a star-strewn sky – seen as clearly from the Yangtze delta as if I had been on Mount Everest, for there was no atmospheric pollution in rural China then – or of the agonized screams of a neighbor who was dying of meningitis, or of our cook's report at breakfast that an infant had been left on our doorstep during the night in its parents' desperate hope that we would adopt and feed it, my earliest memories all carry overtones of life, death, and the things that matter most. Happy memories tumble in quickly – dew between the toes of my bare feet at the start of an incomparably beautiful summer's day is one that remains surprisingly vivid – but as far as I can make out these come from shallower strata of memory. When I came upon the title of de Chirico's painting, "Nostalgia for the Infinite," it presented itself as the signature for my life.

In due course my childhood ruminations took on the outlines of the Protestantism that I assimilated from my parents *cum lacte*, as the Romans said: with my mother's milk. I am grateful for this heritage, whose details have changed but whose premises have not, for to have been launched on life with the assurance that we are in caring hands and that in gratitude for that fact we should try to bear one another's burdens, strikes me as a priceless inheritance.

As we were the only Westerners in our town, my parents were my only Caucasian role models, so I grew up assuming that missionaries were what American children grew up to be. This had me coming to the United States for college thinking it was to acquire the credentials that would take me back to China in my parents' footsteps, but I had not reckoned on the West's dynamism. America was exciting, to the point that within two weeks I had shelved all thoughts of returning to China. No vocational crisis occurred, however, for instead of being a missionary I would be a minister. That resolve lasted for two years when, in my junior year in college – Central Methodist College in Fayette, Missouri – ideas took over and I decided to teach rather than preach. Both vocational shifts occurred smoothly, for throughout them my eye remained on the Big Picture. I wanted to know the final nature of things: reality's deepest structure and what follows from that structure for maximizing the human potential.

While I was in college, theology presented itself as the window onto the Big Picture, but in graduate school at the University of Chicago, philosophy displaced it for seeming to have the wider purview. As for which of philosophy's metaphysical systems was true, naturalism seemed at first to be the obvious choice. Naturalism was tailor-made for science, and science was what distinguished the West from sleepy traditional civilizations. I had caught glimpses of its prowess back in China as I watched townsfolk line up for the smallpox vaccinations my father annually administered. Health was only one of science's valuable deliverances, and naturalism was the metaphysics that fitted science best. John Dewey was the "Jesus" of naturalism and Alfred North Whitehead its "Saint Paul."

There could not have been a more fanatical zealot for naturalism than Huston Smith the graduate student at the University of Chicago, but shortly before I exited that university my naturalistic worldview collapsed like a house of cards. The collapse occurred in a single night through a book on mysticism that had fallen into my hands. Mysticism had scarcely figured in my education, but when it was placed before me undismissively, I saw it as true. There is a reality other than the one that science and common sense – a workable definition of naturalism – set before us, and it is more exciting by every standard that can be invoked. It is more ultimate, more powerful, more awesome, more significant, and more mysterious. My instructors had taught me that Plato's Allegory of the Cave was a brilliant piece of speculation, and yes, magnificent poetry too, but the book I was reading presented it as true. Or rather, as true as words can make out when (through the use of allegory and metaphor) they attempt to describe things that are beyond their reach. I can still feel the electricity of that discovery. Plato tells us that when he thought of the Sun that shines eternally outside the cave of everyday existence, "first a shudder runs through me, and then the old awe creeps over me." Move over, I found myself exclaiming. You have company.

I completed my dissertation perfunctorily, for I needed the union card to teach, but once my diploma was firmly in hand I turned to mysticism seriously. I soon discovered that its fundamental dichotomy – between this world and another world, *samsara* and *nirvana*, the profane and the sacred – needed to be elaborated, and that its consummate elaboration was the Great Chain of Being, the conception of the world as composed of an infinite number of links ranging in hierarchical order from the meagerest kind of existence through every possible grade up to the *ens perfectissimum*, the Perfect Being at its summit.

When the reader comes to the description of my first entheogen experience, the point of this biographical prelude will be glaringly evident. To the best of my ability, it establishes the "set" – to repeat, the psychological makeup through which my experiences of the entheogens, and my thoughts about them as well, have been filtered. There remains the matter of the "setting," which is to say, the circumstances in which I have encountered the substances, and I will devote the second half of this Introduction to that subject.

Setting

The trail goes back to the book that sprung me from my naturalism. In referring to that book, I deliberately withheld its title for fear that it would raise false expectations. One man's meaning is another man's mush, and this holds for the same individual at different stages of his life. Apparently, on the night that I read the book in question my mind had reached the state of a saturated solution which needed but the shock of the right contact for it to recrystallize in a form that startled me. The book I was reading applied that contact, but I have never gone back to it, feeling sure that (as my thoughts have changed) I would now find it disappointing. Still, there is no point in playing cat-and-mouse: the book was Gerald Heard's *Pain, Sex and Time*. There is another reason for mentioning its name, for its author turned out to figure importantly in the road that led me to the entheogens.

Today Gerald Heard is not widely remembered, but at mid-century he was known for having written a best-selling detective story, *A Taste of Honey*, and (to the cognoscenti) as the thinker who had moved his friend Aldous Huxley from the cynicism of his early, *Brave New World* period, to the mysticism of *The Perennial Philosophy*. Before immigrating with Huxley to the United States, Heard was science commentator for the British Broadcasting Company; H. G. Wells said at the time that he was the only man he bothered to listen to on the wireless. Part of the excitement of Heard's writings derived from the way he drew on his BBC background to cite scientific discoveries that seem to support the mystical worldview. After completing my doctorate I read everything he had written, whereupon I determined to meet the man. I wrote to him in care of his publisher and received a reply postmarked "Trabuco Canyon, California," which he explained was in the Los Angeles area.

I made the journey and spent a memorable twenty-four hours with Heard at what turned out to be a retreat center he had founded. As I was leaving he asked if I had met Aldous Huxley, adding that "he's interested in our kinds of things." The prospect of meeting Aldous Huxley at my young age staggered me, and I pursued the lead eagerly. A meeting was arranged by phone, and I returned to Denver having had a second unforgettable encounter, this one an afternoon with Huxley and his wife, Maria, in their hideaway cabin in the Mojave Desert.

An important consequence of my Los Angeles safari was my discovery of the importance that both Heard and Huxley attached to meditation. My Protestantism had taught that if I lived decently I would meet God beyond the grave, but the mystics claimed that God could be found in this life. In a general way I had encountered that belief in the mystical writings I had started to study, but somehow it didn't sink in until I found that Heard was meditating six hours a day to realize God, and that he had founded his retreat center, Trabuco College, for precisely that purpose; Huxley had spent six months there, dividing his time between meditating and writing *The Perennial Philosophy*. Vedanta (the philosophical expression of Hinduism as taught in America by monks of the Ramakrishna order) had sparked Heard's project, for he and Huxley had found those monks to be the most serious and knowledgeable mystics around. (Swami Prabavananda, the director of the Vedanta Society in Hollywood at the time, was the model for the enlightened swami in Somerset Maugham's novel *The Razor's Edge*.) When Heard learned that I was moving from the University of Denver to Washington University, he gave me the name of the swami who headed the Saint Louis Vedanta Society. That swami, Swami Satprakashananda, introduced me to meditation, and for twenty years – ten in Vedanta and ten in Zen training – it was my primary spiritual practice.

With disappointing results, I have to confess. I do not regret those years, and continue to meditate each day, but it does more to strengthen my life's trajectory and call me back to the here and now than it does to produce mystical visions and altered states of consciousness. As a direct experience of God was what I most wanted during those two decades – friends twitted me about whoring after the Absolute – when Huxley's *Doors of Perception* appeared, the mescaline it reported sounded like a Godsend – literally. Like me, Huxley was a poor visualizer – "even the pregnant words of poets do not evoke pictures in my mind; no hypnogogic visions greet me on the verge of sleep," he wrote – yet mescaline overcame that disability and introduced him to "the flow of beauty to heightened beauty, from deeper to ever deeper meaning." Perhaps it could do the same for me.

It took six years to find out. When those years were up, in the fall semester of 1960, Huxley joined the faculty of the Massachusetts Institute of Technology (where I was then teaching) for a semester as Distinguished Visiting Professor of the Humanities. It was the same semester in which Timothy Leary joined the faculty of Harvard University for a three-year appointment as Research Professor in its Center for Personality Research. On his way to that appointment, Leary had ingested seven mushrooms by the side of a swimming pool in Cuernavaca, and, astounded by their effects, he chose as his first Harvard project researching the potentials of psychoactivating chemicals for correcting behavior disorders.

A mile and a half down the Charles River, Aldous Huxley was an obvious resource. When I told Huxley of my interest in the matter, he gave me Leary's phone number and we arranged to meet for lunch at the Harvard Faculty Club. Getting down to business, we pulled out our date books to schedule a session with mescaline. Several tries wouldn't work for one or the other of us, whereupon Leary flipped past Christmas and (with the faintest trace of a mischievous smile, as I remember the scene) asked, "What about New Year's Day?"

It proved to be a prophetic way to enter the "psychedelic sixties."

Empirical Metaphysics

As I noted in my Introduction, my initiation into the entheogens took place in 1961 under the auspices of the Center for Personality Research at Harvard University as part of a project directed by Professor Timothy Leary to determine if a certain class of virtually nonaddictive mind-altering chemicals – mescaline, psilocybin, and LSD – could facilitate behavior change in desirable directions. Such changes are not easy to gauge. Subjective reports are notoriously unreliable, but two populations do lend themselves to statistical measurement. Six months after an entheogen experience, is a paroled prisoner still on the streets or back behind bars, and is the recovered alcoholic still off the bottle? Such were the kinds of questions that the study hoped to answer, but it was necessary to start from scratch, for this was the first concerted effort to study these substances scientifically. (At one point Freud had hopes for cocaine, but he soon abandoned them, and besides, cocaine falls into a different class of drugs because it is addictive.) Accordingly, the first step was to get some idea of the range and kinds of experiences the drugs occasion when given in a supportive atmosphere. Volunteers were solicited to establish a data bank of phenomenological reports. Subjects were screened to rule out those with psychological problems, and precise doses of one of the three drugs being investigated were administered. A physician or psychiatrist was invariably present, with an antidote ready should it be needed – chapter 7 of this book reports the only case I witnessed when one was used. Every effort was made to keep the sessions unstressful. Flowers and music were encouraged, and subjects were invited to surround themselves with meaningful artifacts – family photos, candles, icons, incense – if they chose to do so. Often the "laboratory" was the subject's own living room, and family and friends were welcome to be present. A follow-up report was required in which the subject was asked to describe the experience and retrospective feelings about it.

What follows is the report I turned in. Ralph Metzner got wind of it and included it in the anthology he published, The Ecstatic Adventure.

New Year's Day, 1961. Eleanor (who now answers to the name Kendra) and I reached the home of Dr. Timothy Leary in Newton, Massachusetts, about 12:30 P.M. Present in addition to Leary were Dr. George Alexander, psychiatrist, and Frank Barron, on sabbatical from the department of psychology at the University of California, Santa Cruz.

After coffee and pleasantries, Tim sprinkled some capsules of mescaline onto the coffee table and invited us to be his guest. One, he said, was a mild dose, two an average dose, and three a large dose. I took one; Eleanor, more venturesome, took two. After about half an hour, when nothing seemed to be happening, I too took a second capsule.

After what I estimate to have been about an hour, I noticed mounting tension in my body that turned into tremors in my legs. I went into the large living room and lay down on its couch. The tremors turned into twitches, though they were seldom visible.

It would be impossible for me to fix the time when I passed into the visionary state, for the transition was imperceptible. From here on time becomes irrelevant. With great effort I might be able to reconstruct the order in which my thoughts, all heavily laden with feelings, occurred, but there seems to be no point in trying to do so.

The world into which I was ushered was strange, weird, uncanny, significant, and terrifying beyond belief. Two things struck me especially. First, the mescaline acted as a psychological prism. It was as if the layers of the mind, most of whose contents our conscious mind screens out to smelt the remainder down into a single band we can cope with, were now revealed in their completeness – spread out as if by spectroscope into about five distinguishable layers. And the odd thing was that I could to some degree be aware of them all simultaneously, and could move back and forth among them at will, shifting my attention to now this one, now another one. Thus, I could hear distinctly the quiet conversation of Tim and Dr. Alexander in the adjoining study, and follow their discussion and even participate in it imaginatively. But this leads to the second marked feature. Though the five bands of consciousness – I say five roughly; they were not sharply divided and I made no attempt to count them – were all real, they were not of equal importance. I was experiencing the metaphysical theory known as emanationism, in which, beginning with the clear, unbroken Light of the Void, that light then fractures into multiple forms and declines in intensity as it devolves through descending levels of reality. My friends in the study were present in one band of this spectrum, but it was far more restricted than higher bands that were in view. Bergson's notion of the brain as a reducing valve struck me as accurate.

Along with "psychological prism," another phrase occurred to me: empirical metaphysics. Plotinus's emanation theory, and its more detailed Vedantic counterpart, had hitherto been only conceptual theories for me. Now I was *seeing* them, with their descending bands spread out before me. I found myself amused, thinking how duped historians of philosophy had been in crediting the originators of such worldviews with being speculative geniuses. Had they had experiences such as mine (subsequent chapters of this book suggest that they *had* had such experiences) they need have been no more than hack reporters. But beyond accounting for the origin of these philosophies, my experience supported their truth. As in Plato's myth of the cave, what I was now seeing struck me with the force of the sun, in comparison with which everyday experience reveals only flickering shadows in a dim cavern.

How could these layers upon layers, these worlds within worlds, these paradoxes in which I could be both myself *and* my world and an episode could be both momentary *and* eternal – how could such things be put into words? I realized how utterly impossible it would be for me to describe such things tomorrow, or even right then to Tim or Eleanor. There came the clearest realization I have ever had as to what literary genius consists of: a near-miraculous talent for using words to transport readers from the everyday world to things analogous to what I was now experiencing.

It should not be assumed from what I have written that the experience was pleasurable. The accurate words are significance and terror.* In *The Idea of the Holy*, Rudolf Otto describes awe as a distinctive blend of fear and fascination, and I was experiencing at peak level that paradoxical mix. The experience was momentous because it showed me range upon range of reality that previously I had only believed existed and tried without much success to imagine. Whence, then, the terror? In part, from my sense of the utter freedom of the psyche and its dominion over the body. I was aware of my body, laid out on the couch as if on an undertaker's slab, cool and slightly moist. But I also had the sense that it would reactivate only if my spirit chose to reenter it. Should it so choose? There seemed to be no clear reason for it to do so. Moreover, could it reconnect if I willed it to? We have it on good authority that no man can see God and live – the sight would be too much for the body to withstand, like plugging a toaster into a power line. I thought of trying to get up and walk across the floor. I suspected that I could do so, but I didn't want to risk forcing this intensity of experience into my physical frame. It might shatter the frame.

Later, after the peak had passed and I had walked a few steps, I said to Tim, "I hope you know what you're playing around with here. I realize I'm still under the influence and that things probably look different from your side, but it looks to me like you're taking an awful chance in these experiments. Objective tests might reveal that my heart has been beating normally this afternoon, but there *is* such a thing as people being frightened to death. I feel like I'm in an operating room, having barely squeaked through an ordeal in which for two hours my life hung in the balance."

I have said nothing about the visual. Where it was important,

---

* Years later when I came upon Rilke's *Duino Elegies* I realized that he must have been sensing something like what I was experiencing when he wrote,

> ...*Beauty is nothing*
> *but the beginning of terror, which we still are just able to endure,*
> *and we are so awed because it serenely disdains*
> *to annihilate us.*
>
> (Stephen Mitchell's translation)

it was abstract. Lights such as never were on land or sea. And space – not three or four dimensions but more like twelve. When I focused visually on my physical surroundings, I tended to be uninterested. Shapes and colors, however intensified, had little to contribute to the problem that obsessed me, which was what this experience implied for the understanding of life and reality. So I regarded the visual as largely an intrusive distraction and tended to keep my eyes closed. Only twice did physical forms command my attention. Once was when Dr. Alexander induced me to look at the pattern a lampshade was throwing on a taupe rug. That *was* extraordinary; the shapes stood out like three-dimensional blocks. They also undulated like writhing serpents. The other time was involuntary, when the Christmas tree, its lights unlit, suddenly jumped out at me. It had been in my visual field much of the afternoon, but this was transfiguration. Had I not been in the room throughout, I would have said that someone had re-trimmed the tree, increasing its tinsel tenfold. Where before there was a tree with decorations, now there were decorations with a clotheshorse of a tree to support them.

Interactions with Eleanor, who had dived inward and was reliving important phases of her childhood, form a happy but separate and essentially personal story. Around 10:30 P.M. we drove back to our incomparable, never-more-precious children who were sleeping as if the world was as it had always been, which it definitely was not for us. Neither of us fell asleep until about five, whereupon we slept until around nine. I was definitely into the cold that had been coming on, but my head was clear.

Do Drugs Have Religious Import?

For several years following my initiation, the entheogens were the center of my reflective and social life. Reflectively, to have become overnight
a visionary – one who not merely believes in the existence of a more
momentous world than this one but who has actually visited it – was
no small matter. How could what felt like an epochal change in my life
have been crowded into a few hours and occasioned by a chemical? I
knew how my M.I.T. colleagues – Hans-Lukas Teuber, its renowned
experimental psychologist, and its equally legendary professor of micro-
biology, Jerome Lettvin – would answer that question. The mescaline
had scrambled the synapses in the nerve connections of my brain,
creating irregular associations between its centers for vision, alarm,
euphoria, and excitement, et cetera, et cetera – we get the idea. I was
not persuaded. Still, if chemistry does not tell the whole story, what is
that story? And what part do chemicals, replacing angels as divine
intermediaries, play in it?

Questions like these assaulted me with an urgency that reconstructed
my social life. Family and friends remained in place, but beyond those
I sought out associates who shared my compulsion to talk about and
understand our shared secret. This is the stuff of which churches are
made, and within the Harvard Project an ad hoc "church" emerged. Its
glue was our resistance to epiphenomenal, reductionistic explanations
of our revelations, and our certainty – equal to that of Huxley,
Hofmann, Wasson, and William James, the giants in whose footsteps
we thought of ourselves as walking – that it was impossible to close our
accounts with reality without taking these revelations into consideration. What to make of the entheogens was the question, and we
lived for the times when, like Socrates and his friends, we could hang
out together to talk.

The Harvard Project was hospitable. Open-ended, it wanted to explore
the effects of psychoactive chemicals in all promising directions, so our

"church" had its blessing and benefactions. Once every month or so we gathered to take our sacramental in a vaguely ritualistic context – incense, candles, favorite poems, passages from sacred texts, and spontaneous inputs in the style of Quaker meetings. In between those "services" we gathered to talk philosophically. We were but one satellite in Leary's project, which served as an umbrella under which those of its subjects who wanted to follow up on their experiences clustered and networked. An organization sprang up, the International Federation for Internal Freedom, which for ten years published a journal, The Psychedelic Review. *It attracted some notable contributors, among them Robert Graves, Aldous Huxley, Albert Hofmann, and Gordon Wasson.*

Lisa Bieberman and Peter John (who went on to become a Methodist minister) deserve to be mentioned for holding our "church" together; without pay or public recognition, they gave virtually their full time to it. Readers of this book may recognize the names of several other members of our group for the parts they played in the history of the entheogens. Walter Houston Clark, professor of the psychology of religion at Andover-Newton Theological Seminary, became the most ardent crusader for the substances, arguing that they were the only things in sight that could restore the experiential component to the mainstream churches, without which they would not survive. Walter Pahnke's Good Friday Experiment is the subject of chapter 7 in this book; it is difficult to imagine how the history of the entheogens might have been different had he not died in a scuba-diving accident, for he brought to his serious involvement with mysticism the scientific training of a medical doctor and his intention to devote his career to studying the resources of chemicals for religion. Paul Lee, who at the time was Paul Tillich's teaching assistant at Harvard, went on to teach philosophy at the University of California, Santa Cruz, before leaving academia to devote himself fulltime to studying herbs.

The essay that follows sets forth the conclusions I reached about the entheogens in the course of the three years that I was involved with the Harvard Project. Titled "Do Drugs Have Religious Import?" it appeared in the 1 October 1964 issue of The Journal of Philosophy. *I am told that it has been anthologized more times than any other article in that journal, over twenty times to date. I have made a few minor alterations to clarify points that might otherwise be obscure.*

Until six months ago, if I picked up my phone in the Cambridge area and dialed KISS-BIG, a voice would answer, "If-if." These were coincidences: KISS-BIG happened to be the letter equivalents of an arbitrarily assigned telephone number, and I.F.I.F. represented the initials of an organization with the improbable name of the International Federation for Internal Freedom. But the coincidences were apposite to the point of being poetic. "Kiss big" caught the euphoric, manic, life-embracing attitude that characterized this most publicized of the organizations formed to explore the newly synthesized consciousness-changing substances; and the organization itself was surely one of the "iffyest" phenomena to appear on our social and intellectual scene in some time. It produced the first firings in Harvard's history – of professors Timothy Leary and his associate, Richard Alpert – and an ensuing ultimatum to Leary to get out of Mexico in five days; and also "the Miracle of Marsh Chapel," in which, during a two-and-a-half-hour Good Friday service, fifteen theological students and professors ingested psilocybin and were visited by what they generally reported to be the deepest religious experiences of their lives.

Despite the last of these phenomena and its numerous, if less dramatic, parallels, students of religion appear to be dismissing the psychedelic drugs that have sprung to our attention in the sixties as having little religious relevance. The position taken in one of the most forward-looking volumes of theological essays to have appeared in recent years – *Soundings,* edited by A. R. Vidler[1] – accepts R. C. Zaehner's *Mysticism, Sacred and Profane* as having "fully examined and refuted" the religious claims for mescaline which Aldous Huxley sketched in *The Doors of Perception.* This closing of the case strikes me as premature, for it looks as if the drugs have light to throw on the history of religion, the phenomenology of religion, the philosophy of religion, and religious life itself.

1. *Drugs and Religion Viewed Historically*

In their trial-and-error life explorations, peoples almost every-where have stumbled upon connections between vegetables (eaten or brewed) and actions (yogic breathing exercises; fast, whirling-dervish dances; self-flagellations) that induce dramatic alterations in consciousness. From the psychopharmacological standpoint we now understand these states to be the products of changes in brain chemistry. From the sociological perspective we see that they tend to be connected in some way with religion. If we discount the wine used in Christian communion services, the instances closest to us in time and space are the Peyote sacra-ment of the Native American Church and Mexico's two-thou-sand-year-old tradition of using sacred mushrooms, the latter rendered in Aztec as "God's Flesh," a striking parallel to "the body of our Lord" in the Christian Eucharist. Further away are the *soma* of the Hindus, the *haoma* and hemp of the Zoroastrians, Dionysus the Greek who "everywhere taught men the culture of the vine and the mysteries of his worship and everywhere was accepted as a god,"[2] the *benzoin* of Southeast Asia, Zen's tea whose fifth cup purifies and whose sixth "calls to the realm of the immortals,"[3] the *pituri* of the Australian aborigines, and probably the mystic *kykeon* that was drunk at the climactic close of the sixth day of the Eleusinian Mysteries.[4] There is no need to extend the list, as a reasonably complete account is given in Philippe de Felice's comprehensive study of the subject, *Poisons Sacrés, Ivresses Divines*.

More interesting than the fact that consciousness-changing de-vices have been linked with religion is the possibility that they may actually have initiated many of the religious perspectives which, taking root in history, continued after their entheogenic origins were forgotten. Bergson saw the first movement of Hindus and Greeks toward "dynamic religion" as associated with the "divine rapture" found in intoxicating beverages,[5] and more recently Robert Graves, Gordon Wasson, and Alan Watts have suggested that most religions have arisen from such chemically induced theophanies. Mary Barnard is the most explicit proponent of this thesis. "Which was more likely to happen first," she asks; "the spontaneously generated idea of an afterlife in which the disembodied soul, liberated from the restrictions of time and space, experiences eternal bliss, or the accidental discovery of hallucinogenic plants that give a sense of euphoria, dislocate the center of consciousness, and distort time and space, making them balloon outward in greatly expanded vistas?"[6] Her own answer is that "the latter experience might have had an almost explosive effect on the largely dormant minds of men, causing them to think of things they had never thought of before. This, if you like, is direct revelation." Her use of the subjunctive "might" renders this formulation of her answer equivocal, but she concludes her essay on a note that is categorical: "Looking at the matter coldly, unintoxicated and unentranced, I am willing to prophesy that fifty theobotanists working for fifty years would make the current theories concerning the origins of much mythology and theology as out-of-date as pre-Copernican astronomy."

This is an important hypothesis – one which must surely engage the attention of historians of religion for some time to come. But as I am content here to forego prophecy and limit myself to the points where the drugs surface in serious religious study, I shall not pursue Ms. Barnard's thesis. Having tagged what appears to be the crux of the historical question, namely the extent to which drugs not merely duplicate or simulate theologically sponsored experiences but generate or shape theologies themselves, I turn to phenomenology.

2. Drugs and Religion Viewed Phenomenologically

Phenomenology attempts a careful description of human experience. The question that drugs pose for the phenomenology of religion, therefore, is whether the experiences they induce differ from religious experiences reached without them and, if so, how.

Even the Bible notes that substance-altered psychic states bear *some* resemblance to religious ones. Peter had to appeal to a circumstantial point – the early hour of the day – to defend those who were caught up in the Pentecostal experience against the charge that they were merely drunk: "These men are not drunk, as you suppose, since it is only the third hour of the day" (Acts 2:15); and Paul initiates the comparison when he admonishes the Ephesians not to "get drunk with wine, but to be filled with the spirit" (Ephesians 5:18). Are such comparisons, which have counterparts in virtually every religion, superficial? How far can they be pushed?

Not all the way, students of religion have thus far insisted. With respect to the new drugs, Professor R. C. Zaehner has drawn the line emphatically. "The importance of Huxley's *Doors of Perception*," he writes, "is that in it the author clearly makes the claim that what he experienced under the influence of mescaline is closely comparable to a genuine mystical experience. If he is right, the conclusions are alarming."[7] Zaehner thinks that Huxley is not right, but I believe that it is Zaehner who is mistaken.

There are, of course, innumerable drug experiences that have no religious features; they can be sensual as readily as spiritual, trivial as readily as transforming, capricious as readily as sacramental. If there is one point about which every student of psychoactivating agents agrees, it is that there is no such thing as *the* drug experience per se – no experience that the drugs, as it were, secrete. Every experience is a mix of three ingredients: drug, set (the psychological makeup of the individual), and setting (the social and physical environment in which it is taken). But given the right set and setting, the drugs can induce religious experiences that are indistinguishable from such experiences that occur spontaneously. Nor need the sets and settings be exceptional. The way the statistics are currently running, it looks as if from one-fourth to one-third of the general population will have religious experiences if they take certain drugs under naturalistic conditions, meaning conditions in which the researcher supports the subject but does not interfere with the direction the experience takes. Among subjects who have strong religious proclivities, the proportion of those who will have religious experiences jumps to three-fourths. If such subjects take the drugs in religious settings, the percentage soars to nine out of ten.

How do we know that the experiences these people have really are religious? We can begin with the fact that they say they are. The "one-fourth to one-third of the general population" figure is drawn from two sources. Ten months after they had had their experiences, 24 percent of the 194 subjects in a study by the California psychiatrist Oscar Janiger characterized their experiences as having been religious.[8] Thirty-two percent of the seventy-four subjects in Ditman and Hayman's study reported, looking back on their LSD experience, that it looked as if it had been "very much" or "quite a bit" a religious experience; 42 percent checked as true the statement that they "were left with a greater awareness of God, or a higher power, or ultimate reality."[9] The statement that three-fourths of subjects having religious "sets" will have religious experiences comes from the reports of sixty-nine religious professionals who took the drugs while the Harvard project was in progress.[10]

In the absence of (a) a single definition of religious experience generally acceptable to psychologists of religion, and (b) foolproof ways of ascertaining whether actual experiences exemplify any definition, I am not sure there is a better way of telling whether the experiences of the 333 men and women involved in the above studies were religious than by their reports that they seemed so to them. But if more rigorous methods are preferred, they exist; they have been utilized, and they confirm the conviction of the man in the street that drug experiences can indeed be religious. In his doctoral study at Harvard University, Walter Pahnke worked out a typology of religious experience (in this instance, mystical experience) based on classic reports that Walter Stace included in his *Mysticism and Philosophy*. Pahnke then administered psilocybin to fifteen theology professors and students (half of the total population of thirty) in the setting of a Good Friday service. The drug was given in a "double-blind" experiment, meaning that neither Dr. Pahnke nor his subjects knew which fifteen were getting psilocybin and which fifteen received placebos to constitute a control group. Subsequently the subjects' reports of their experiences were rated independently by three former schoolteachers on the degree (strong, moderate, slight, or none) to which each report evinced the nine traits of mystical experience that Stace enumerates. The results showed that "those subjects who received psilocybin experienced phenomena which were indistinguishable from, if not identical with, the categories defined by our typology of mysticism."[11]

With the thought that the reader might like to test his or her own powers of discernment on the question being considered, I insert here a simple test I gave to members of the Woodrow Wilson Society at Princeton University. I presented them with two accounts of religious experiences, one drug-occasioned, the other not, and asked them to guess which was which.

I

Suddenly I burst into a vast, new, indescribably wonderful universe. Although I am writing this over a year later, the thrill of the surprise and amazement, the awesomeness of the revelation, the engulfment in an overwhelming feeling-wave of gratitude and blessed wonderment, are as fresh, and the memory of the experience is as vivid, as if it had happened five minutes ago. And yet to concoct anything by way of description that would even hint at the magnitude, the sense of ultimate reality . . . this seems such an impossible task. The knowledge which has infused and affected every aspect of my life came instantaneously and with such complete force of certainty that it was impossible, then or since, to doubt its validity.

II

All at once, without warning of any kind, I found myself wrapped in a flame-colored cloud. For an instant I thought of fire . . . the next, I knew that the fire was within myself. Directly afterward there came upon me a sense of exultation, of immense joyousness accompanied or immediately followed by an intellectual illumination impossible to describe. Among other things, I did not merely come to believe, but I saw that the universe is not composed of dead matter, but is, on the contrary, a living Presence; I became conscious in myself of eternal life. . . . I saw that all men are immortal: that the cosmic order is such that without any peradventure all things work together for the good of each and all; that the foundation principle of the world . . . is what we call love, and that the happiness of each and all is in the long run absolutely certain.

On the occasion referred to, twice as many students (46) answered incorrectly as answered correctly (23). I bury the correct answer in an endnote to enable the reader to test himself on the question if he wishes to do so.[12]

Why, in the face of this considerable evidence, does Zaehner hold that drug experiences cannot be authentically religious? There appear to be three reasons:

1. His own experience was "utterly trivial." This of course proves that not all drug experiences are religious, but not that none is.

2. He thinks the experiences of others that appear religious to them are not truly so. Zaehner distinguishes three kinds of mysticism: nature mysticism, in which the soul is united with the natural world; monistic mysticism, in which the soul merges with an impersonal absolute; and theistic mysticism, in which the soul confronts the living, personal God. He concedes that drugs can induce the first two species of mysticism, but not its supreme instance, the theistic. As proof, he analyzes Huxley's experience as recounted in *The Doors of Perception* to show that it produced at best a blend of nature and monistic mysticism. Even if we were to accept Zaehner's evaluation of the three forms of mysticism, Huxley's case (and indeed Zaehner's entire book) would prove only that not every mystical experience induced by the drugs is theistic. Insofar as Zaehner goes beyond this to imply that drugs do not and cannot induce theistic mysticism, he not only goes beyond the evidence but proceeds in the face of it. James Slotkin reports that the Peyote Indians "see visions, which may be of Christ Himself. Sometimes they hear the voice of the Great Spirit.

Sometimes they become aware of the presence of God and of those personal shortcomings which must be corrected if they are to do His will."[13] And G. M. Carstairs, reporting on the use of *bhang* in India, quotes a Brahmin as saying, "It gives good *bhakti*," *bhakti* being precisely Hinduism's theistic way of relating to the divine.[14]

3. There is a third reason why Zaehner might doubt that drugs can induce genuinely mystical experiences. Zaehner is a Roman Catholic, and Roman Catholic doctrine teaches that mystical rapture is a gift of grace and as such can never be brought under human control. This may be true; certainly the empirical evidence cited does not preclude the possibility of a genuine ontological or theological difference between natural and drug-induced religious experiences. At this point, however, we are considering phenomenology rather than ontology, description rather than truth-claims, and on this level there is no difference. Descriptively, drug experiences cannot be distinguished from their natural religious counterparts. When the current philosophical authority on mysticism, W. T. Stace, was asked whether the drug experience is similar to the mystical experience, he answered, "It's not a matter of its being *similar to* mystical experience; it is mystical experience."

What we seem to be witnessing in Zaehner's *Mysticism, Sacred and Profane* is a reenactment of the age-old pattern in the conflict between science and religion. Whenever a new controversy arises, religion's first impulse is to deny the disturbing evidence science has produced. Seen in perspective, Zaehner's refusal to admit that drugs can induce experiences descriptively indistinguishable from spontaneous ones is a current counterpart of the seventeenth-century theologians' initial refusal to accept the evidence for the Copernican revolution. When the fact that drugs can trigger religious experiences becomes incontrovertible, discussion will move to the more difficult question of how this fact is to be interpreted. That question leads beyond phenomenology into philosophy.

3. Drugs and Religion Viewed Philosophically

Why do people reject evidence? Presumably because they find it threatening. Theologians are not the only professionals who can be defensive. In his *Personal Knowledge*,[15] Michael Polanyi recounts the way the medical profession ignored such palpable facts as the painless amputation of human limbs performed before their own eyes in hundreds of successive cases, concluding that the subjects were impostors who were either deluding their physicians or colluding with them. One physician, Esdaile, carried out about three hundred major operations painlessly under mesmeric trance in India, but neither in India nor in Great Britain could he get medical journals to print accounts of his work. Polanyi attributes this closed-mindedness to "lack of a conceptual framework in which their discoveries could be separated from specious and untenable admixtures."

The "untenable admixture" in the fact that psychotomimetic drugs can induce religious experiences is its apparent implication: that religious disclosures are no more veridical than psychotic ones. For religious skeptics, this conclusion is of course not untenable at all; it fits perfectly with their thesis that *all* religion is at heart an escape from reality. Psychotics avoid reality by retiring into make-believe dream worlds; what better evidence could there be that religious visionaries do the same than the fact that their visions can be chemically induced as well? Marx appears to have been more than metaphorically accurate in proposing that religion is the "opiate" of the people. And Freud too was more right than he realized. He "never doubted that religious phenomena are to be understood only on the model of the neurotic symptoms of the individual."[16] He should have said "psychotic symptoms."

So the religious skeptic is likely to reason. What about the religious believer? Convinced that religious experiences are basically veridical, can he admit that psychoactive drugs can occasion them? To do so he needs (to return to Polanyi's words) "a conceptual framework in which [the discoveries can] be separated from

25

specious and untenable admixtures," the "untenable admixture" here being the conclusion that religious experiences are in general delusory.

One way to effect the separation would be to argue that, despite phenomenological similarities between natural and drug-induced religious experiences, they are separated by a crucial *ontological* difference. Such an argument would follow the pattern of theologians who argue for the "real presence" of Christ's body and blood in the bread and wine of the Eucharist despite their admission that chemical analysis, confined as it is to the level of "accidents" rather than "essences," would not disclose this presence. But this distinction will not appeal to many today, for it turns on an essence-accident metaphysics which is not widely accepted. Instead of fighting a rear-guard action by insisting that if drug and non-drug religious experiences cannot be distinguished empirically there must be some transempirical factor that distinguishes them and renders the drug experience profane, I wish to explore the possibility of validating drug-induced religious experiences on grounds that they come up with the same basic claims about reality that religions always do.

To begin with the weakest of all arguments, the argument from authority, William James (whom I class among the religious for his sensibilities) did not discount *his* insights that occurred while his brain chemistry was altered. The paragraph in which he retrospectively evaluates his nitrous oxide experiences has become classic, and I quote it here for its pertinence to the point under consideration.

> One conclusion was forced upon my mind at that time, and my impression of its truth has ever since remained unshaken. It is that our normal waking consciousness, rational consciousness as we call it, is but one special type of consciousness, whilst all about it, parted from it by the filmiest of screens, there lie potential forms of consciousness entirely different. We may go through life without suspecting their existence; but apply the requisite stimulus, and at a touch they are there in all their completeness, definite types of mentality which probably somewhere have their field of application and

adaptation. No account of the universe in its totality can be final which leaves these other forms of consciousness quite disregarded. How to regard them is the question – for they are so discontinuous with ordinary consciousness. Yet they may determine attitudes though they cannot furnish formulas, and open a region though they fail to give a map. At any rate, they forbid a premature closing of our accounts with reality. Looking back on my own experiences, they all converge toward a kind of insight to which I cannot help ascribing some metaphysical significance.[17]

To this argument from authority, I add two arguments that try to provide something by ways of reasons. Drug experiences that assume a religious cast tend to have fearful and/or beatific features, and my hypotheses relate to these two features of the experience.

Beginning with the ominous, "fear of the Lord" awe-full feature, I have already registered in the frontispiece of this book Gordon Wasson's account, which (being short) I reenter here. "Ecstasy! In common parlance ecstasy is fun. But ecstasy is not fun. Your very soul is seized and shaken until it tingles. After all, who will choose to feel undiluted awe? The unknowing vulgar abuse the word; we must recapture its full and terrifying sense."[18]

Emotionally the drug experience can be like having forty-foot waves crash over you for several hours while you cling desperately to a life raft which may be swept from under you at any moment. It seems quite possible that such an ordeal, like any experience of a close call, could awaken fundamental sentiments respecting life, death, and destiny, and trigger the "no atheists in foxholes" effect. Similarly, as the subject emerges from the ordeal and realizes that he will not be permanently insane as he had feared, he may experience waves of overwhelming relief and gratitude like those that patients recovering from critical illnesses frequently report. Here is one such report.

It happened on the day when my bed was pushed out of doors to the open gallery of the hospital. I cannot now recall whether the revelation came suddenly or gradually; I only remember finding myself in the very midst of those wonderful moments, beholding life for the first time in all its young intoxication of loveliness, in its unspeakable joy, beauty, and importance. I cannot say exactly what the mysterious change was. I saw no new thing, but I saw all the usual things in a miraculous new light – in what I believe is their true light. I saw for the first time how wildly beautiful and joyous, beyond any words of mine to describe, is the whole of life. Every human being moving across that porch, every sparrow that flew, every branch tossing in the wind, was caught in and was a part of the whole mad ecstasy of loveliness, of joy, of importance, of intoxication of life.[19]

If we do not discount religious intuitions because they are prompted by battlefields and physical crises; if we regard the latter as "calling us to our senses" more often than they seduce us into delusions, need comparable intuitions be discounted simply because the crises that trigger them are of an inner, psychic variety?

Turning from the fearful to the beatific aspects of the drug experience, some of the latter may be explainable by the hypothesis just stated; that is, they may be occasioned by the relief that attends the sense of escape from high danger. But this hypothesis cannot possibly account for all of the blissful episodes that chemicals occasion for the simple reason that the positive episodes often come first, or to persons who experience no negative episodes whatever. Dr. Sanford Unger of the National Institute of Mental Health reports that among his subjects "50 to 60% will not manifest any real disturbance worthy of discussion, yet around 75% will have at least one episode in which exaltation, rapture, and joy are the key descriptions."[20] How are we to account for the drug's capacity to induce peak experiences, such as the following, which are not preceded by fear?

A feeling of great peace and contentment seemed to flow through my entire body. All sound ceased and I seemed to be floating in a great, very very still void or hemisphere. It is impossible to describe the overpowering feeling of peace, contentment, and being a part of goodness itself that I felt. I could feel

my body dissolving and actually becoming a part of the goodness and peace that was all around me. Words can't describe this.
I feel an awe and wonder that such a feeling could have occurred
to me.[21]

Consider the following argument: Like every other form of
life, human nature has become distinctive through specialization.
Human beings have specialized in developing a cerebral cortex.
The analytic powers of this instrument are a standing wonder, but
the instrument seems less able to provide people with the sense
that they are meaningfully related to their environment: to life,
the world, and history in their wholeness. As Albert Camus describes the situation, "If I were a cat among animals, this life
would have a meaning, or rather this problem would not arise, for
I should belong to this world. I would *be* this world to which I am
now opposed by my whole consciousness."[22] Note that it is
Camus's consciousness that opposes him to his world. The drugs
do not knock this consciousness out, but while they leave it
operative they also activate areas of the brain that normally lie
below its threshold of awareness. One of the clearest objective
signs that the drugs are taking effect is the dilation they produce
in the pupils of the eyes, and one of the most predictable subjective signs is the intensification of visual perception. Both of these
responses are controlled by portions of the brain that lie deep,
further to the rear than the mechanisms that govern consciousness. Meanwhile we know that the human organism is joined to
its world in innumerable ways that our senses do not pick up –
through gravitational fields, bodily respiration, and the like: the
list could be multiplied until the human skin begins to look more
like a traffic maze than a boundary. Perhaps the deeper regions of
the brain which evolved earlier and are more like those of the
lower animals – "If I were a cat I should belong to this world" –
can sense this relatedness better than can the cerebral cortex
which now demands our attention. If so, when the drugs re-
arrange the neurohumors that chemically transmit impulses
across synapses between neurons, human consciousness and its
submerged, intuitive, ecological awareness might for a spell become interlaced. This is, of course, no more than a hypothesis,

but how else are we to account for the extraordinary incidence under the drugs of that kind of insight the keynote of which James described as "invariably a reconciliation"? "It is as if," he continues, "the opposites of the world, whose contradictoriness and conflict make all our difficulties and troubles, were melted into one and the same genus, but one of the species, the nobler and better one, is itself the genus, and so soaks up and absorbs its opposites into itself."[23]

4. Drugs and Religion Viewed "Religiously"

Suppose that drugs can induce experiences indistinguishable from religious experiences and that we can respect their reports. Do they shed any light, I now ask, not on life, but on the nature of the religious life?

One thing they may do is throw religious experience itself into perspective by clarifying its relation to the religious life as a whole. Drugs appear to be able to induce religious experiences; it is less evident that they can produce religious lives. It follows that religion is more than a string of experiences. This is hardly news, but it may be a useful reminder, especially to those who incline toward "the religion of religious experience"; which is to say toward lives bent on the acquisition of desired states of experience irrespective of their relation to life's other demands and components.

Despite the dangers of the "faculty psychology" that was in vogue in the first half of this century, it remains useful to regard human beings as having minds, wills, and feelings. One of the lessons of religious history is that to be adequate, a faith must activate all three components of human nature. Overly rationalistic religions grow arid, and moralistic ones grow leaden. Those that emphasize experience have their comparable pitfalls, as evidenced by Taoism's struggle (not always successful) to keep from degenerating into quietism, and the vehemence with which Zen Buddhism insists that once students have attained *satori*, they must be driven out of it and back into the world. The case of Zen is especially pertinent here, for it pivots on an enlightenment experience – *satori*, or *kensho* – which some (but not all) Zen Buddhists say resembles the LSD experience. Alike or different, the point is that Zen recognizes that unless the experience is joined to discipline, it will come to naught.

> Even the Buddha continued to sit. Without *joriki*, the particular power developed through *zazen* [seated meditation], the vision of oneness attained in enlightenment in time becomes clouded and eventually fades into a pleasant memory instead of remaining an omnipresent reality shaping our daily life. To be able to live in accordance with what the mind's eye has revealed through *satori* requires, like the purification of character and the development of personality, a ripening period of *zazen*.[24]

If the religion of religious experience is a snare and a delusion, it follows that no religion that fixes its faith primarily in substances that induce religious experiences can be expected to come to a good end. What promised to be a shortcut will prove to be a short circuit; what began as a religion will end as a religious surrogate. Whether chemical substances can be helpful adjuncts to faith is another question. The Peyote-using Native American Church seems to indicate that they can be; anthropologists give this church a good report, noting among other things that its members resist alcohol better than do nonmembers.[25] The conclusion to which the evidence seems currently to point is that it is indeed possible for chemicals to enhance the religious life, but only when they are set within the context of faith (conviction that what they disclose is true) and discipline (exercise of the will toward fulfilling what the disclosures ask of us).

Nowhere today in Western civilization are both of these conditions met. Faith has declined in churches and synagogues, and the counterculture lacks discipline. This might lead us to forget about the drugs, were it not for the fact that the distinctive religious emotion, and the one that drugs can unquestionably occasion – Otto's *mysterium tremendum, majestas, mysterium fascinans;* in a phrase, the phenomenon of religious awe – seems to be declining sharply. As

31

Paul Tillich said in an address to the Hillel Society at Harvard several years ago:

> The question our century puts before us is: Is it possible to regain the lost dimension, the encounter with the Holy, the dimension that cuts through the world of subjectivity and objectivity and goes down to that which is not world but is the mystery of the Ground of Being?

Tillich may be right; this may be the religious question of our century. For if (as I have argued) religion cannot be equated with religious experiences, neither can it long survive their absence.

Psychedelic Theophanies and the Religious Life

During the three years that followed the writing of the preceding essay, the hopes that had attended Timothy Leary's Harvard project began to fade. Albert Hofmann's LSD: My Problem Child pretty much tells the story. Hofmann, the discoverer of LSD, had had high hopes for his compound (mainly as an adjunct to psychiatry), but he became alarmed when it proved to be no more containable than other drugs and was pounced on for recreational use. A drug culture emerged as a component of the counterculture that arose to protest the war in Vietnam, the backlash to the civil rights movement that led to the assassination of Martin Luther King, and disillusionment with a science that had created the atomic bomb, napalm, and environmental pollution. Timothy Leary was fired from Harvard University for transgressing the agreement that undergraduate students would not be involved in his program. Irish rebel that he was at heart, he joined the counterculture, became its idol, and coined its famous slogan, "Turn on, tune in, drop out."

These developments called for a reassessment of my initial, rather optimistic appraisal of the promise entheogens hold for religion. Everything I had said in my Journal of Philosophy essay still struck me as true, but I came to feel that the distinction between religious experiences and the religious life needed to be emphasized more than it was in that piece. This next essay, which appeared in Christianity and Crisis in 1967, supplies that missing emphasis. Written later in the sixties, it contains more social history – the history of that tumultuous decade – than do the other essays in this book. As with the other essays, I have made minor changes in the original text.

Psychedelic experiences can be religious. Subjects often say that they are, and their reports can read like accounts of classic theophanies.

What concerns me here is their staying power. No theophany is certain to retain its force – backsliding, falling from grace, and the psalmist's lament, "restore unto me the joy of my salvation," are not discoveries of the psychedelic age. And psychedelic theophanies can have *some* staying power: among alcoholics (Saskatchewan), lawbreakers (Laguna Beach, California), severe neurotics (Spring Grove State Hospital, Maryland), and terminal cancer patients (Chicago and Spring Grove). Nevertheless, I suspect that psychedelic religious experiences are having, and for the foreseeable future will continue to have, less faith-filled carryover than those that occur spontaneously.

I say this less for inductive than for deductive reasons. With too little available data at this point for an inductive conclusion, my pessimism derives from the following syllogism:

Major premise: Religious history suggests that for theophanies to take hold, certain conditions must obtain.

Minor premise: Those conditions are lacking in the psychedelic movement.

Conclusion: Psychedelic theophanies are not likely at this juncture of history to have substantial staying power.

What are the conditions that are needed for theophanies to take hold? The most important one is conviction, carrying over into the non-drug state, that the insights that emerge in the theophany are true.

That a theophany's disclosures seem true while the theophany is in progress follows by definition: it would not be a theophany but some other kind of experience were it to be otherwise. As René Daumal says: "At that moment comes *certainty*. Speech must now be content to wheel in circles around that bare fact." The experience's content is certain because doubts could enter only from the perspective of this world, which world pales before (where it is not obliterated by) the world into which the see-er has stepped.

34

Except in the tragic case of psychotics, however, this world eventually reasserts itself and its claims press hard upon us, which claims in our culture challenge the validity of pharmacological theophanies. The two foremost Western models of the mind are those of hard science (artificial intelligence and its chemical counterpart) and soft science (depth psychology with Freudianism in the lead). Both of these stand ready to explain chemically assisted convictions in ways that explain them away.

Artificial Intelligence and the Freudian Model

Is one moved in the course of a psychedelic experience to the conviction that everything is perfect just as it is; that (as Hakuin put it in his "Song in Praise of Zazen") "this earth on which we stand / is the promised Lotus Land / and this very body is the body of the Buddha"? The cyberneticist will tell us why. What happens to produce that "realization" is that in the neurological reshuffling that LSD occasions, the conviction center of our brain flip-flops to yes/green/go while being wired to the euphoria center. Meanwhile, contravening impressions are short-circuited and shut out. This last is an important point, for it challenges the all-too-common, too vague, too uncritical claim that psychedelics expand consciousness. The balloon image that that phrase suggests is less apposite than that of a microscope. Does a microscope enlarge our vision? Yes, by enabling us to see deeper into nature; but concomitantly no, for it shuts out everything but the microscopic object at which we are looking. According to the artificial-intelligence account, everything seems wonderful because at the moment in question euphoria fills our horizon. The entire world seems wonderful because the world has been collapsed to include only the rose-tinted things we have in mind at the moment.

As for the noetic property of the experience – the conviction that what one witnesses are not subjective phantasms but realities that exist objectively in the world, William James listed this as one of the four marks of mystical experience, but artificial intelligence explains it away on grounds that novel experiences hit us with exceptional force because they are not glazed over by habituation, the loss in vividness that repetition breeds.

The Freudian proceeds by a different route, but he too can discredit the experiences of ego-transcendence, the dissolution of the subject/object dichotomy, and the peace that passeth understanding that entheogens occasion. They are variations of the "oceanic feeling" that results when subjects regress psychologically to their mothers' wombs.

I do not defend these contemporary models of the mind; I merely point out that they saturate contemporary thinking to the point that even those who consciously reject them are imprinted by them to a large degree. This makes it difficult to accept psychedelic theophanies at face value, but is not history studded with examples of sects that have managed to survive while holding beliefs that challenge reigning conventions?

The point is well taken, and it takes me to my second reason for doubting the staying power of psychedelic experiences. History shows that minority faiths are viable, but only when they are cradled in communities that are solid and structured enough to constitute what in effect are churches. To date, the psychedelic movement shows no signs of having within it the makings of such a church. Sporadic "happenings" in makeshift quarters, and periodic gestures toward institutionalization, do not challenge this assertion; they confirm it by their ineffectiveness.

I say "no signs of the makings of a church," but perhaps I should qualify that in one respect. The psychedelic movement does have a charismatic leader: a man of intelligence, culture, and charm who is completely self-assured and apparently absolutely fearless. When Arthur Kleps, head of a branch of the short-lived Neo-American Church, testified before the Special Senate Judiciary Subcommittee on Narcotics that "we regard Dr. Timothy Leary with the same special love and respect as was reserved by the early Christians for Jesus, by Muslims for Mohammed, and by Buddhists for Gautama," we sensed the presence of charisma, the magnetism of a person who is regarded by his followers as an embodiment of spiritual power.

A charismatic leader is a great asset to a movement, but his presence is not sufficient to insure its success. And the psychedelic movement possesses other features which, if religious history provides grounds for prediction, augur against its becoming a genuine church. It lacks a social philosophy. It is antinomian. And, ignoring the Taoist adage to know ten things but tell only nine, it draws no line between the exoteric (what can appropriately be made public) and the esoteric, which should be reserved for the initiated.

I begin with the first of these three lacks.

A flawed social program

The psychedelic movement lacks a blueprint for relating itself to society. That it rejects the claims of mainstream culture is glaringly apparent. "You must quit your attachments to American society," wrote Leary in the first installment of his column syndicated by the counterculture's *East Village Other* and carried by the *L.A. Free Press*, the *Fifth Estate*, and *The Paper*.

Many early Christians adopted a comparable stance. The author of The New Testament's First Letter of John admonishes his readers not to "love the world or the things in the world" (2:15). He condemns the world for "its sensuality, superficiality and pretentiousness, its materialism and its egoism" (C. H. Dodd's summary in *The Johannine Epistles*). I have not heard psychedelic spokesmen criticize today's establishment for its sensuality, but otherwise the parallel is exact, as are those between some of Leary's writings and Tertullian's directives to the Christian church as it confronted the Roman Empire.

Tertullian	*Leary*
Political life is to be eschewed.	It is impossible to live conventionally on this planet without joining the antilife social systems. So drop out.

Tertullian	*Leary*
Trade is scarcely fitting for a servant of God, for apart from covetousness there is no real motive for engaging in it.	American social institutions lust for material things, so quit your job. For good.
Academicians, typified by the philosophers, have nothing in common with the disciples of heaven. They corrupt the truth. They seek their own fame. They are talkers rather than doers.	Present educational methods are neurologically crippling and antagonistic to your cellular wisdom. Quit school. For good.

Equally striking is the parallel between the reason Clement gives for why Christians should sit loose to society – they represent a new race of people – and the claims of the psychedelic prophets who regard persons under thirty as a new breed, a mutation in human evolution.

These similarities are impressive, but there is an important difference. Early Christians were apocalyptic; they expected the imminent end of history through divine intervention. This gave them a philosophy of history that underwrote their opposition to a social order. The psychedelic movement has no such philosophy.

Obviously, apocalypticism is not the only alternative to a prevailing social system; there is the possibility of improvements that people themselves effect. If the psychedelic leaders had a social philosophy that pointed in this direction, they would be (like Muhammad) not just rebels but revolutionaries. They have no such philosophy.

There is a third possibility. Neither apocalyptic nor revolutionary, the psychedelic movement might be utopian in seeking to create humane enclaves within a society that as a whole is considered to be beyond redemption. The utopian tradition has a respectable history in the West; the nineteenth century witnessed more than two hundred utopian ventures in the United States alone. But to date the psychedelic movement has failed to create a viable utopian community. Several attempts have been made, but they have been short-lived.

If the psychedelic movement were apocalyptic, revolutionary, or utopian, it would present an alternative to the status quo. Being none of these, its social message comes down to "Quit school. Quit your job. Drop out." The slogan is too negative to command respect.

Antinomianism

The psychedelic movement is antinomian. Derived from the Greek word meaning "law," antinomianism is the belief that it is possible to advance in virtue to a point where one stands above the law and is entitled to lay aside its commands in the name of a higher morality.

An historical example that sheds light on the psychedelic movement's antinomian tendencies and the problems that attend that stance is the Oneida Community, a New York product of the religious revival that swept America in the 1830s. Its founder, John Humphrey Noyes, became convinced as a result of his religious awakening and subsequent studies that the second coming of Christ did not lie in the future but had occurred at the close of the Apostolic Age. He found the corollaries of this conclusion to be far-reaching. First, original sin having been effectively eradicated by Christ's unrecognized return, nothing remained in human nature to keep people from living perfectly right now. Second, once (through the exercise of understanding and resolve) human beings do begin to live perfectly, no external guides for living can rival their own consciences and intelligence.

Noyes was absolutely convinced that salvation without the law presented the central idea of Christ's gospel. But, as his biographer, G. W. Noyes, points out, he found the doctrine "exceedingly liable to be perverted," and the perversions produced three disruptive forces in his community: sexual irresponsibility, anarchy, and lethargy. Noyes's descriptions of these problems read like a warning to the psychedelic movement. According to the Oneida Community's founder, right action had two essential components, right intent and intelligence. Since these internal monitors might conflict with external law, right action without freedom from external law was a contradiction in terms. Hence Noyes and his followers, though brought up in the strictest school of New England morality, declared themselves free from law. But here a new danger appeared. In escaping from the law, many of the Perfectionists, like the medieval mystics, fell into antinomianism. Antinomianism takes different forms according to the temperamental susceptibilities of its subjects. In those inclined to sensuality it takes the form of lasciviousness; in those whose leading trait is self-esteem, it takes the form of anti-organization; in those of an indolent disposition it takes the form of lethargy. During the prevalence of the antinomian aberration in 1835–1836 it seemed as though the Oneida Community would be completely given over to anarchy and imbecility. The Perfectionists did not abandon the principle of freedom from law, but they were brought gradually to the conviction that even the spiritually-minded in the present stage of human development needed to be restrained by moral forces which, though consistent with personal freedom, were nevertheless in effect equivalent to the law.

I commend to the psychedelic movement the example of John Humphrey Noyes. Here was a man who, in the name of religious convictions, advocated practices in comparison with which drug-taking seems tame. In the interests of spiritual eugenics he advocated what the law defined then and continues to define as adultery and bastardy. Yet – and here is the genius of the man – on this socially scandalous platform and in the face of enormous public opposition, he founded a community of several hundred persons that prospered financially (we still use its silverware) and spanned three generations, as against the average three-year life-span for utopian communities. An important factor in his success was his facing up to the tension between freedom and antinomianism in a manner more substantial than I find in his contemporary counterparts.

Comparable lessons come from Asia, the source of much of the psychedelic movement's inspiration. The West picks up Zen's endorsements of freedom and spontaneity enthusiastically, and Zen does indeed celebrate these qualities extravagantly. But careful reading of the record shows that it presents them as the crown of years of arduous discipline. Kenneth Ch'en's *Buddhism in China* points out that advancement in the hierarchy of Ch'an Buddhism was contingent on a dozen or so years of intensive study of, and discipline in, the *vinaya*, the first and moral disciplines basket of the three-basket *Tipitaka*, a work so detailed in its moral injunctions that it would fill about a dozen good-sized volumes in a western library. D. T. Suzuki picks up the thread and adds that even with this requirement in place, Ch'an and Zen still had to exercise great vigilance to keep from degenerating into stultifying passivity, the heresy known as quietism. To guard against this dry rot, Ch'an leaders introduced the requirement that monks work. The first rule of Ch'an monastic life was "A day of no work is a day of no eating."

This prompts me to ask if the corollary of "turn on" and "tune in" has to be "drop out"? To appeal to Asian traditions in support of antinomianism – be the traditions Ch'an, Zen, Tibetan Buddhism, or even Tantra in its Hindu and Buddhist versions – is to take their names in vain.

The esoteric/exoteric divide

To argue that there are things in religion that are best kept secret cuts against our democratic grain, yet tested religions do so argue.* There are pearls which, cast before swine, will be damaged themselves (by trampling) or damage the swine (should the swine eat them). In its early centuries, Christianity reserved a number of

---

* As do tested philosophies at times. A major Platonic scholar, J. N. Findlay, says that the two following sentences from Plato's Seventh Letter should be put at the head of every translation of Plato's works: "The publicizing of those secrets [with which that letter is concerned] I do not deem a boon for men, excepting for those initiates who are able to discover them with no more than a given hint. For the others it would produce a stupid derision or else a self-glorification in a mistaken idea that they have eaten wisdom with spoons."

its dogmas for those who had undergone probationary instruction and been baptized. The promise that was exacted of them, "I will not speak of thy mysteries to thine enemies," still appears in orthodox Christian liturgies.

Asia followed the same route. India developed the guru system in which disclosures to disciples are calibrated to the disciples' capacities to comprehend them. In the *Bhagavad Gita*, Krishna forbids imparting higher knowledge to those who are not ready for it, and in the *Katha Upanisad*, Yama tests Nachiketa's fitness in various ways before consenting to impart his highest teachings. In the *Taittiriya Upanisad*, Varuna puts off his son Bhrigu four times (with instructions to kindle the fire of his soul by aspiration, self-discipline, and meditation) before imparting to him the knowledge of Brahman. In raja yoga, *yama* and *niyama*, preliminary rules of discipline and purification are held to be indispensable prerequisites. India honors higher states of consciousness fully as much as today's psychedelic proponents do, but insists that if they are accessed by persons who are unprepared for them, one of two things will happen. Either (as I have said) the subject will be damaged, or the significance of the experience will be missed and the encounter trivialized. Thus either the subject is damaged or the *dharma* is damaged, usually both. The psychedelic movement pays lip service to these dangers by advising screening and preparing subjects, but on the whole it honors the esoteric/exoteric distinction only perfunctorily.

Inability to integrate the psychedelic experience with daily life is not without precedent. In the Ch'an/Zen tradition, early texts (as John Blofeld has pointed out) tend to cite *satori* as the goal of training. Later texts do not. The reason seems clear. When *satori* first arrives, its momentousness is likely to make it seem ultimate, the be-all and end-all of existence. As life goes on, however, one recognizes that this is not the case. Routine reasserts itself, and one discovers that even those who have had powerful *satoris* sometimes misbehave. At this point there enters the realization that comes to be stressed increasingly in later texts. In those texts *satori* is not the goal; it is the first major hurdle in the unending endeavor to work the *satori* experience into the fabric of one's daily life until one's entire life takes on a *satoric* quality. "Drawing water, hewing wood – this is the supernatural power; this the marvelous activity."[1]

Despite the fact that I do not see within the psychedelic movement the makings of a viable church, I hope that (as legal use of the entheogens seems destined for the immediate future to be restricted to research) "religious research" will not be considered a contradiction in terms. If a sincere group wishing to use the entheogens for genuinely religious purposes were permitted to do so while qualified observers kept close check on what happens to the group and in the individual lives of its members, the results would at least be interesting, and might be instructive.

That is my conclusion. I append a short postscript.

Strange things seem to be happening to human religiousness in our time, especially among the young. On the one hand, students are making a left end run around the prophetic, this-worldly wing of institutional religion to tackle directly such issues as Vietnam, racial justice, and the problems of poverty. This has been evident for several years.

What is new is that they are now making a right end run around the priestly, other-worldly wing of institutional religion to link up with Zen, Tibetan, and Asian gurus of wide variety, Native American spirituality, channeling, and the New Age cornucopia generally, including pharmacological mysticism. Theological supernaturalism is being replaced by psychological supernaturalism, defined as belief in the existence of paranormal powers and their deliverances.

Whether the current chapter of human religiousness is being written more in churches and ecumenical councils or on college campuses and in experimental communes is a question whose answer is blowing in the wind.

Historical Evidence: India's Sacred Soma

This essay steps back from the current scene to see what history can tell us about the entheogens. Preceding chapters have touched on that question, but this one zeroes in on an important chapter in religious history – Hinduism in its formative period – to treat it as a case study.

The contextual facts are these: Among the gods of the Vedic pantheon, Soma appears to have been the most revered. His home was a plant, and in the holiest of rituals priests ingested the god by drinking a brew that was made from this plant. Somewhere along the way the plant's identity was lost, and any Indologist who retrieved it was assured of a permanent place in the annals of his discipline. It came as a surprise, therefore, when the prize went to an amateur – a retired banker named R. Gordon Wasson.

I considered the subject sufficiently important to give a summer to researching it, and this essay reports my findings. Its copious footnotes show that (like the second essay in this book) it was written for an academic journal; titled "Wasson's SOMA: A Review Article," it appeared in the December 1972 issue of the Journal of the American Academy of Religion.[1] I pause for a moment to indulge myself. Because my best-known work, The World's Religions, is an undergraduate text that appeared early in my career, I have had to struggle against the fear – self-imposed perhaps, but real nonetheless – of being written off by my colleagues as a popularizer. It has, therefore, encouraged me no end that the foremost linguist of my time, Roman Jakobson, called this essay "a magnificent survey," and that one of the two leading historians of religion in my generation, Wilfred Cantwell Smith (the other was Mircea Eliade) credited it with being "a model of a piece: superbly organized, marvelously informative, engagingly written, and altogether exactly right."

If I were writing it today, I would have to temper my claim that Gordon Wasson solved the soma enigma conclusively. The quarter-

century that has elapsed has brought new criticisms of his arguments, and rival candidates for the soma plant have been proposed. I continue to think that Wasson's arguments for his candidate are the strongest in the field, but the debate continues.

To get an immediate sense of the relevance of Wasson's work for this book, I suggest that the reader begin by reading the long footnote that appears on page 51. It is as compelling an account of the entheogenic experience as I know.

I have spent so much time recently reviewing the work of others that I am growing impatient to get on with my own pursuits, but the thesis here considered is important enough to warrant another detour. Moreover, the excursion is bound to prove interesting, for it leads through one of the most colorful intellectual exploits of our century.

Having mentioned both importance and interest, let me begin with the former. Alfred North Whitehead is reported to have remarked that Vedanta is the most impressive metaphysics the human mind has conceived.[2] The extent to which it may have influenced our own western outlook after Alexander's invasion of India does not concern us here; what is at issue is its origins.

Etymologically and otherwise, Vedanta is "the culmination of the Vedas," and the Vedas derive, more than from any other single identifiable source, from Soma.* Would it not be useful, then, to

---

* As this statement may seem excessively categorical, I give my reasons for it. Soma enjoys a special place in the Vedic pantheon. I will indicate the specifics of that place shortly, but let me acknowledge that its position warrants my allegation only when supported by recognition of the extent to which the Upanisadic metaphysics could have been facilitated by the entheogen that Soma was, and in the Vedas was exclusively. My arguments supporting this recognition fall into three categories: personal experience, the role of the entheogens in engendering religious perspectives generally, and the distinctive character of the Soma experience in Vedic religion.

(a) Personal experience. I quote from the account of my own first ingestion of an entheogen, mescaline. "Another phrase came to me: 'empirical metaphysics.' The emanation theory and elaborately delineated layers of Indian cosmology and psychology had hitherto been concepts and inferences. Now they were objects of direct, immediate perception. I saw that theories such as these were required by the experience I was having. I found myself amused, thinking how duped historians of philosophy had been in crediting those who formulated such worldviews with being speculative geniuses. Had they had experiences such as mine they need have been no

46

know what Soma was? Not particularly, India herself seems to have
answered, judging from her scholars' lack of interest in identifying

more than hack reporters. Beyond accounting for the origin of these philosophies,
my experience supported their truth. As in Plato's myth of the cave, what I was now
seeing struck me with the force of the sun in comparison with which normal experience was flickering shadows on the wall" ("Empirical Metaphysics," in Ralph Metzner, ed., *The Ecstatic Adventure* [New York: The Macmillan Company, 1968], p. 73).

(b) On the role of entheogens in occasioning religious purviews generally, I quote
again, as I did in an earlier essay, Mary Barnard who asks, "Which was more likely
to happen first: the spontaneously generated idea of an afterlife in which the disembodied soul, liberated from the restrictions of time and space, experiences eternal
bliss, or the accidental discovery of hallucinogenic plants that give a sense of euphoria, dislocate the center of consciousness, and distort time and space, making
them balloon outward in greatly expanded vistas? The [latter] experience might have
had an almost explosive effect on the largely dormant minds of men, causing them
to think of things they had never thought of before. [I interrupt to note that in reading for the present review I came across a pointed support of Ms. Barnard's conjec-
ture, specifically the part connecting the concept of an afterlife to hallucinogens.
Concerning certain Algonquin Indians in the region of Quebec, Father Charles Lallemand wrote in 1626, "They believe in the immortality of the Soul; and in troth they
so assert that after death they go to Heaven, where they do eat Mushrooms" (21).]
Looking at the matter coldly, unintoxicated and unentranced, I am willing to prophesy that fifty theo-botanists working for fifty years would make the current theories
concerning the origins of much mythology and theology as out-of-date as pre-
Copernician astronomy," *The Mythmakers* (Athens, Ohio University Press, 1966), pp.
21–22, 24. On the same theme, by the author of the book under review: "As man
emerged from his brutish past there was a stage in the evolution of his awareness
when the discovery of [an indole] with miraculous properties was a revelation to
him, a veritable detonator to his soul, arousing in him sentiments of awe, reverence,
gentleness and love, to the highest pitch of which mankind is capable, all those sentiments and virtues that mankind his ever since regarded as the highest attribute of
his kind. It made him see what this perishing mortal eye cannot see. What today is
resolved into a mere drug was for him a prodigious miracle, inspiring in him poetry
and philosophy and religion" (1:162). (Numbers preceding colons refer to numbered
items in the bibliography; those following colons to page numbers therein.)

(c) Finally, on the specific place of the entheogen experience in Vedic religion,
these words by Daniel Ingalls, Wales Professor of Sanskrit at Harvard University,
written to register a perception that came to him on reading through Book IX, the
Soma Book, of the Rig-Veda after reading Wasson's book here under review. "Soma
and Agni represent the two great roads between this world and the other world.
They are the great channels of communication between the human and the divine."
But, Ingalls goes on to note, there is a difference. "The Agni hymns seek for a har-
mony between this world and the sacred, but are always aware of the distinction.
The Soma hymns, on the other hand, concentrate on an immediate experience.
There is no myth, no past, no need, for harmony. It is all here, all alive and one. The
Soma experience was always an extraordinary event, exciting, immediate, transcend-
ing the logic of space and time."

the lost plant – that characteristic Indian casualness toward history again. Western scholars, by contrast, have been curious from the first. In the two centuries since Indology became an academic discipline in Europe, forty-three candidates for Soma were proposed in the nineteenth century, and in the twentieth the number rose to a total of over one hundred. Any Indologist who settled the issue would have been assured of a permanent place in the annals, not only of Indian and religious scholarship, but of historical scholarship generally. Most ranking scholars had abandoned the quest as hopeless.

This is where the story picks up, for when the answer arrives – and it will be the burden of my review that it has arrived – it comes not from a Sanskritist, Indologist, or academician of any stripe. It comes from outside the world of professional scholarship altogether, from an amateur – a retired banker, and a high-school dropout at that. But more. Let the master clue be one of the most improbable lines in all Sacred Writ: "Fullbellied the priests piss the sacred Soma"; a line which, verging on scatology, had regularly thrown the pundits into confusion and leveled the exegetes. Let the discovery surface in a bibliophile's dream that is a story in itself – printed in limited edition on handmade paper, the book became a collector's item overnight. Finally, let the subject fall squarely in taboo domain – the chaotic, puzzling, passion-filled world of the "psychedelics," with all that word has come to mean to America in the last fifteen years – and the reader can see why I felt that my own work could wait. The immediate occasion for my review is the appearance of *SOMA* in a popular edition, but it is also time for a general stock-taking, because the three years since the book's initial publication have allowed time for reviews to appear in the major critical journals.

I. Where Things Stood

In the pantheon the Aryans brought with them when they swept into Afghanistan and the Indus Valley in the second millenium B.C.E., Soma occupied a unique position. Indra with his thunderbolt was more commanding, and Agni evoked the awe that fire so readily inspired before the invention of matches made it common-place. But Soma was special, partly (we may assume) because one could become Soma through ingestion, but also because of what one then became: "We have drunk Soma and become immortal." The Soma hymns are vibrant with ecstasy. It appears to be virtually the only plant man has deified; the Mexican Indians regard mush-rooms, *peyotl*, and morning glories as "god's flesh" or in other ways mediators of the divine, but the plants do not figure in their pan-theons. The crucial Mandala IX consisting of 114 of the Rig-Veda's 1,028 hymns is dedicated exclusively to Soma, as are six other hymns, but his significance extends far beyond these hymns in which he is invoked in isolation. "Soma saturates the Rig-Veda" (7:169); the entire corpus is "shot through with Soma." "The Soma sacrifice was the focal point of the Vedic religion," writes W. D. O'Flaherty, adding,

> Indeed, if one accepts the point of view that the whole of In-dian mystical practice from the *Upanisads* through the more mechanical methods of yoga is merely an attempt to recapture the vision granted by the Soma plant, then the nature of that vision — and of that plant — underlies the whole of Indian reli-gion, and everything of a mystical nature within that religion is pertinent to the identity of the plant. (4:95)

Louis Renou once said that the whole of the Rig-Veda is encapsu-lated in the themes Soma presents.

In the course of the Soma sacrifice dried plants were steeped in water and their juice pounded out with stones and wooden boards covered with bull hides. This juice was then forced through wood-en filters and blended with milk, curds, barley water, ghee, and oc-casionally honey. To the priests who drank the holy brew it is said to have given strength, magnitude, and brilliance. "One has only to read the Soma hymns," Daniel Ingalls observes, "to grant some truth to the claim" (15:15).

Then, even as the last parts of the Vedas were being composed, Soma disappears. The Brämanas, codified around 800 B.C.E., contain no mention of it. Reverence for the god persisted; his sacrifice continues to be performed right down to today. But surrogates replaced the original plant. For nearly three thousand years, Soma retreats to the mountain fastnesses from whence it came. Like a yogi in training, deliberately isolated so his austerities won't be interrupted, Soma drops out of history – to the historians' dismay, as I earlier remarked.

II. Enter Gordon Wasson

In certain respects Gordon Wasson was an unlikely candidate for the discoverer. He knew no Sanskrit, had no special interest in India, and his years were against him; born in 1898, he was already in his sixties and had retired from his banking career when he turned to Soma. But it goes without saying that he didn't just stumble on his find. He was equipped for the search – ideally so, we can say with wisdom of hindsight. To begin with, he was intelligent. His career bears this out from beginning to end. Without having completed high school he was appointed to teach English at Columbia University. Turning from that to journalism, he served as financial reporter for the *New York Herald Tribune* until his uncanny sense of the business world caused J. P. Morgan and Company to take him on and advance him, in time, to a vice-presidency. And atop this basic intelligence Wasson had erected a specialist's repertoire. Though he was neither scholar nor scientist by profession, there was a field in which he was a master, and it was the one that proved to be decisive: ethnomycology. Assisted by his wife, Valentina Pavlovna, a pediatrician who died in 1959, his work in this area had led to (a) rediscovery of *teonanactl,* the sacred mushroom of Mexico[3] and the worldwide attention it subsequently received; (b) publication in 1957 of a monumental two-volume treatise, *Mushrooms, Russia and History (3),* which argued the possibility of the mushroom cult being man's oldest surviving religious institution; (c) reputation as founder of a science of "ethnomycology," a name analogous to "ethnobotany"; (d) appointment as Research Fellow (later Honorary Research Fellow) of the Botanical Museum of Harvard University; and (e) Honorary Research Fellow of the New York Botanical Garden and Life Member of the Garden's Board of Managers.

These talents alone might have sufficed, but the longer one ponders the Soma discovery, the more facets of Gordon Wasson appear relevant until one has to remind oneself that it wasn't the preordained purpose for which he was born. Though advanced in years when he hit the Soma trail, his health and zest for research, including fieldwork, had held up; ten years later he continues to sleep in a sleeping bag on a screened porch the year 'round in Connecticut temperatures that can dip to fifteen degrees below zero. His depth-exploration of the Mexican mushroom – for years he and his wife spent their annual vacation in joint expeditions with the great French mycologist, Roger Heim – had made him directly, experientially knowledgeable about entheogens and the way they can function in a religious setting.* Even the careers Wasson pursued on his

---

* I do not consider this an incidental resource. I find it not only aetiologically natural but metaphysically apposite that Soma's identity should have been discovered by an initiate – not, to be sure, in the Soma cult itself, but in a western counterpart. We both search and find according to our sensibilities, a point which (if I may be pardoned a personal reference) has been borne in on me by the one empirical discovery of my career. Had I not possessed, first, a musical ear which alerted me immediately to the fact that in the Gyüto (Tibetan) chanting I was in the presence of something subtly astonishing; and second, a musical temperament which required that I get to the bottom of what had so moved me, the "important landmark in the study of music," which *Ethnomusicology* (January 1972) credited the find as being, would not have been forthcoming. Something comparable, I am certain, was at work in Wasson's discovery of Soma. To indicate what it was, I quote at length from Wasson's response to the sacred mushroom of Meso-America which he came upon twenty years earlier.

"When we first went down to Mexico, we felt certain, my wife and I, that we were on the trail of an ancient and holy mystery, and we went as pilgrims seeking the Grail. To this attitude of ours I attribute such success as we have had. A simple layman, I am profoundly grateful to my Indian friends for having initiated me into the tremendous Mystery of the mushroom.

"In the uplands of southern Mexico the rites take place now, in scattered dwellings, humble, thatched, without windows, far from the beaten track, high in the mountains of Mexico, in the stillness of the night, broken only by the distant barking of a dog or the braying of an ass. Or, since we are in the rainy season, perhaps the Mystery is accompanied by torrential rains and punctuated by terrifying thunderbolts.

"Then, indeed, as you lie there bemushroomed, listening to the music and seeing the visions, you know a soul-shattering experience. The orthodox Christian must accept by faith the miracle of Transubstantiation. By contrast, the mushroom of the

way to Soma were only seeming detours. English and journalism
gave him a feel for language which was to grace his report when it

Aztecs carries its own conviction; every communicant will testify to the miracle that
he has experienced. 'He who does not imagine in stronger and better lineaments,
and in stronger and better light than his perishing eye can see, does not imagine at
all,' Blake writes. The mushroom puts many (if not everyone) within reach of this
state. It permits you to see, more clearly than our perishing mortal eye can see, vistas
beyond the horizons of this life, to travel backwards and forwards in time, to enter
other planes of existence, even to know God. It is hardly surprising that your emotions are profoundly affected, and you feel that an indissoluble bond unites you with
the others who have shared with you in the sacred *agape*. All that you see during this
night has a pristine quality: the landscape, the edifices, the carvings, the animals –
they look as though they had come straight from the Maker's workshop. This new-
ness of everything – it is as though the world had just dawned – overwhelms you
and melts you with its beauty. Not unnaturally, what is happening to you seems to
you freighted with significance, beside which the humdrum events of the everyday
are trivial. All these things you see with an immediacy of vision that leads you to say
to yourself, 'Now I am seeing for the first time, seeing direct, without the intervention of mortal eyes.'

"And all the time that you are seeing these things, the priestess sings, not loud,
but with authority. You are lying on a *petate* or mat; perhaps, if you have been wise,
on an air mattress and in a sleeping bag. It is dark, for all lights have been extin-
guished save a few embers among the stones on the floor and the incense in a sherd.
It is still, for the thatched hut is apt to be some distance away from the village. In
the darkness and stillness, that voice hovers through the hut, coming now from beyond your feet, now at your very ear, now distant, now actually underneath you,
with strange, ventriloquistic effect. Your body lies in the darkness, heavy as lead, but
your spirit seems to soar and leave the hut, and with the speed of thought to travel
where it listeth, in time and space, accompanied by the shaman's singing. You are
poised in space, a disembodied eye, invisible, incorporeal, seeing but not seen. In
truth, you are the five senses disembodied, all of them keyed to the height of sensitivity and awareness, all of them blending into one another most strangely, until the
person, utterly passive, becomes a pure receptor, infinitely delicate, of sensations. As
your body lies there in its sleeping bag, your soul is free, loses all sense of time, alert
as it never was before, living an eternity in a night, seeing infinity in a grain of sand.
What you have seen and heard is cut as with a burin in your memory, never to be
effaced. At last you know what the ineffable is, and what ecstasy means. Ecstasy! For
the Greeks *ekstasis* meant the flight of the soul from the body. Can you find a better
word than that to describe the bemushroomed state? In common parlance ecstasy is
fun. But ecstasy is not fun. Your very soul is seized and shaken until it tingles. Who
will choose to feel undiluted awe, or to float through that door yonder into the
Divine Presence?

"A few hours later, the next morning, you are fit to go to work. But how unim-
portant work seems to you, by comparison with the portentous happenings of that
night! If you can, you prefer to stay close to the house, and, with those who lived
through the night, compare notes, and utter ejaculations of amazement." (Con-
densed and slightly transposed from 1:149–62.)

appeared,* and banking, being lucrative, enabled him to travel when fieldwork beckoned and to consult the authorities whose diverse areas of expertise – Sanskrit, history, philology, comparative mythology, folklore, art, poetry, literature, ecology, ethnobotany, phytochemistry, and pharmacology – he was to fit with his own mycological knowledge to craft the solution. Also, when it became apparent that the Vedic references would be crucial, he could employ a talented Sanskritist, Wendy Doniger O'Flaherty of the School of Oriental and African Studies of the University of London, to translate the relevant passages. Wasson's comfortable circumstances bear, too, on SOMA as a *de luxe* publication, to which a later section of this review will be devoted. Its author is an aristocrat; every dimension of his life has style.

Finally, it was in Wasson's favor that he was not an academic. We need not go as far as Robert Graves and credit his innocence of a university education with preserving his genius. It is enough to share Professor Ingalls's suspicion, voiced at a testimonial dinner at the Harvard Faculty Club on the occasion of the publication of the book under review, that the specialists, each burrowing deeper and deeper down the narrowing shaft of his own specific competence, would never have discovered Soma's secret. The problem called for an amateur, a man who could approach it with innocence and love and across disciplinary boundaries.

The *Concise Oxford Dictionary* defines "amateur" as "one who is fond of; one who cultivates a thing as a pastime." The French is stronger; my dictionary renders it "lover, virtuoso." Wasson was an amateur mycologist in the French sense. His love and consequent

---

* I content myself with a single example: "Often have I penetrated into a forest in the fall of the year as night gathered and seen the whiteness of the white mushrooms, as they seemed to take to themselves the last rays of the setting sun and hold them fast as all else faded into the darkness. When fragments of the white veil of the fly-agaric still cling to, the cap, though night has taken over all else, from afar you may still see Soma, silver white; resting in his well-appointed birth-place close by some birch or pine tree. Here is *how* three thousand years ago a priest-poet of the Indo-Aryans gave voice to this impression: "By day he appears the color of fire, by night, silver white (IX 97^{9d})." Soma's scarlet coat dominates by day; by night the redness sinks out of sight, and the white patches, silvery by moon and starlight, take over" (4:41–42).

virtuosity respecting the mushrooms rooted back into nothing less decisive than his love for his wife. In August 1927, newly wed and enjoying a vacation in the Catskills, they chanced on a forest floor that was covered with wild fungi. Their responses were exact opposites: he was indifferent, even distrustful, while she was seized by wild glee. Some couples might have left the difference at that, but the Wassons were of an inquiring bent. Examining their difference, they found it to be rooted in a difference between entire peoples. Dr. Wasson, a White Russian who practiced pediatrics in New York, had absorbed almost *cum lacte* (with her mother's milk) a solid body of empirical knowledge about mushrooms and a passionate regard for them; even "worthless" varieties were arranged with moss and stones into attractive centerpieces. By contrast, Gordon, of Anglo-Saxon heritage, had been shielded from the plants. Given to pejoratives like "toadstool" and exaggerated rumors of their toxicity, his people had been as mycophobic as hers had been mycophilic. In Russian literature mushrooms figure in love scenes and pastoral idylls; in English they are emblems of death. For over thirty years the Wassons devoted much of their leisure to dissecting, defining, and tracing this difference until it led to the thesis – supported by comparative philology, mythology, legends, fairy tales, epochs, ballads, historical episodes, poetry, novels, and scabrous vocabularies that are off-limits to proper lexicographers – that at some point in the past, perhaps five thousand years ago, our European ancestors had worshiped a psychoactive mushroom, and that their descendants had divided according to whether the *facinans* (fascination) or the *tremendum* (fear) of its holy power predominated.

Two years after the publication of *Mushrooms, Russia and History* in 1957, Mrs. Wasson died, and Gordon, forced into life changes and with a pension sufficient for his needs, retired from banking and promoted ethnomycology from his hobby into a second career. Soma was not on his docket. He wanted to look into the "mushroom madness" of New Guinea (still unsolved) and why the Maoris of New Zealand share the Eurasian association of mushrooms with lightning. Somewhere down the line he intended to examine India's largely negative attitude toward mushrooms, and this led him to spend some weeks in 1964 at the American Institute of Indian Studies at Poona where he began reading Renou's translation of the Vedas. It proved to be the turning point. During the days that followed, on a freighter to Japan, a number of disjointed things he had learned during forty years of research fell into place. The hypothesis that Soma was a mushroom, specifically the *Amanita muscaria* or fly-agaric,[4] came to view. From that point on it was a matter of corroborating his hypothesis.

III. The Evidence

To enter all the evidence Wasson uncovered in his five ensuing years of concentrated work in the libraries and botanical centers of the United States and Europe, and in the field in Asia, would be to duplicate his book. Instead I shall summarize the evidence he marshals for his conclusion under six points.

1. The references to Soma contain no mention of the leaves, flowers, fruit, seeds, and roots that pertain to chlorophyll-bearing plants. They refer repeatedly to stems and caps.

2. All the color references fit the *Amanita muscaria*. There is no mention of its being green, black, gray, dark, or blue (the colors of vegetation), while the colors that are mentioned conform without exception to the mushroom's cap (bright red), the membrane, unique to the *A. muscaria*, that protects it in its early stages (brilliant white), or its pressed – *sauma* means "to press" – juice (golden or tawny yellow). Wasson makes the latter point by using quotations from the Rig-Veda to caption a series of stunning photographs of the fly-agaric. The color-epithet that is invoked most often is *hari*, which in Sanskrit "seems to have run from red to light yellow" (4:37), always accenting its dazzling and resplendent character which the photographs that Wasson himself took capture brilliantly. "The hide is of a bull [red bulls are favored in India], the dress of sheep" (IX 70[7]). This "dress of sheep," the white membrane, is invoked by a variety of analogies: "He makes from milk

his robe of state" (IX 71²), and "with unfading vesture, brilliant, newly clothed, the immortal [Soma] wraps himself all around. He has taken to clothe himself in a spread-cloth like to a cloud" (IX 69⁵). The mushroom's rupture of its embryonic envelope, too, is noted. "He sloughs off the Asurian colour that is his. He abandons his envelope" (IX 72²). "Like a serpent he creeps out of his old skin" (IX 86⁴⁴ᵉ). The flecks of the veil that cling to the mushroom's crown after the veil bursts give meaning to "he lets his color sweat when he abandons his envelope" (IX 71²).

3. References to shape are equally apposite. The mushroom's head, peering through the undergrowth while still in its white skin, is "the single eye" (IX 9⁴). When its cap is fully formed, it mirrors the vault of heaven and is "the mainstay of the sky." Or again, its curved cap can look like an udder – "the swollen stalks were milked like cows with [full] udders" (VIII 9¹⁹ᵃᵇ) – and its puffy foot like a teat: "The priests milk this shoot like the auroral milch cow" (I 137ᵃᵇ).

4. Soma altered consciousness but was not alcohol; it was an entheogen. The Aryans knew alcohol in the form of *sura*, a beer, but the time allotted for Soma's preparation in the sacrifices precludes fermentation. Moreover, whereas the Vedas generally disapprove of *sura*, noting the muddleheadedness and other bad effects it produces, Soma is not only *aducchuna*, without evil effects; it leads to godliness:

> We have drunk the Soma, we have become immortal, we have arrived at the light, we have found the gods.
>
> What now can the enemy do to harm us, and what malice can mortals entertain? Amplify, O Soma, our lives for the purpose of living.
>
> These splendid waters, granting much, protecting.
>
> Like fire produced by friction, may the waters inflame us! May they cause us to see afar and to have increasing welfare (Rig-Veda, VIII 48).

5. Geography fits. *Amanita muscaria* requires, for host, the north temperate birch forest, and the Indus Valley is bordered by lofty mountains whose altitude compensates for its southern latitude. South of the Oxus River, *A. muscaria* grows only at altitudes of eight thousand feet or more, and this fits with the fact that Soma was confined to mountains. Parts of Afghanistan, where the Aryans resided before continuing their southeastward push, and the Hindu Kush through which they entered the Indian subcontinent, are *A. muscaria* country.

6. Finally, there is the line of the Rig-Veda that I quoted at the beginning of this essay which has priests urinating diluted Soma. The *Amanita* is an entheogen whose vision-producing properties are known to survive metabolic processing. Ritualistic urine-drinking forms a part of a number of fly-agaric ceremonies that have survived to the present in Siberia and elsewhere. As translated by most Indologists, a verse in the Rig-Veda, (IX 74[4]) reads, "The swollen men urinate the on-flowing Soma." There is, in addition, the fact that the Vedas mention a "third filter" for Soma while describing only two; Wasson thinks this third filter could have been the human organism which, there is reason to believe, reduces the nauseous properties of the fly-agaric while retaining for as many as five ingestions the chemical, musicimol, which in the dried mushroom is the entheogenic agent.

IV. Critical Response

Wasson's *SOMA* appeared in 1969; this review is being written three years later. The interval has allowed time for authorities to review the use Wasson makes of their respective fields, and I categorize the most significant of their verdicts.

A. NONCOMMITTAL

F. B. J. Kuiper, Vedist, University of Leiden: "Wasson may be perfectly right in assuming that the original Soma plant was the

Amanita muscaria, but the problem cannot be solved beyond doubt" (18:284).

Winthrop Sargent, critic: "Wasson has given us the most persuasive hypothesis that has yet appeared, but nobody really can say what Soma was" (25).

B. CONFIRMING

Sanskritists and Indologists

Daniel Ingalls, Harvard University: The "basic facts about the Soma plant as described in the Rig-Veda cannot well be accounted for by any of the previous identifications. . . . They are all perfectly accounted for by the identification with the mushroom *Amanita muscaria* or fly agaric. Not all the epithets remarked on by Wasson need be taken just as he takes them, but enough still remains to be convincing. Wasson's identification is a valuable discovery" (14:188).

Stella Kramrisch, Institute of Fine Arts, New York University: "Wasson proves beyond doubt that Soma was prepared from *Amanita muscaria*. He has set right almost three thousand years of ignorance about the 'plant of immortality'" (17).

Wendy Doniger O'Flaherty, University of London: "For long she [O'Flaherty] was skeptical about my thesis, but she now authorizes me [Wasson] to say here today [at the International Congress of Orientalists, Canberra, January 1971] that she is a fullfledged convert" (7:169).

Ulrich Schneider, University of Freiburg: In his book *Der Somaraub des Manu*, 1971, he concludes that Soma is *Amanita muscaria*.

Botanists and mycologists

Albert Pilat in the Swiss bulletin of mycology: "In this interesting and magnificently produced work, the noted American ethnomycologist, R. Gordon Wasson, proves that the religious drug known under the name of 'Soma' is *Amanita muscaria"* (24:11).

Richard Evans Schultes, Botanical Museum Harvard University: "The data fit together as tightly as pieces of an intricate jig-saw puzzle. Wasson provides, so far as I am concerned, incontrovertible proof of the strongest kind that Soma must have been *Amanita muscaria*. Once and for all he has provided the identification" (27:101–5).

Anthropologists

Claude Lévi-Strauss, College de France: "Mr. Wasson's work establishes convincingly that, among all the possible candidates for Soma, *Amanita muscaria* is far and away the most plausible" (20).

Weston La Barre, Duke University: "The closure of linguistic, botanical, ethnographic, and ecological evidence is exhilarating. The identification of soma with *Amanita muscaria* is definite and the Sanskrit puzzle of two millennia, from the *Brahmanas* to this day, can now be regarded as finally solved" (19:371).

Linguists

Calvert Watkins, Harvard University: "I accept Wasson's identification of Soma with *A. muscaria*. I am myself by way of being an amateur mycologist, and in my review article (in preparation for Wolfgang Meid [ed.], *Gedenkschrift für Hermann Güntert* [Innsbruck, 1973]), I hope to show that there is considerably more evidence for his hypothesis in the Rig-Veda, and also in the Iranian, Avestan, data, with which he was not concerned" (from a letter, 19 June 1972, to the author of this review).

Generalists

Robert Graves, poet, mythologist, savant: "Wasson has identified Soma, without any possibility of scientific or scholarly doubt, as the *Amanita muscaria*, or 'fly-agaric'. The argument is as lucid as it is unanswerable. His book satisfies me completely. I congratulate him on his feat" (12:109, 113).

C. REJECTING

John Brough, Professor of Sanskrit, Cambridge University: "It is with regret that I find myself unable to accept that Wasson has proved his theory that the original Vedic Soma was *Amanita muscaria*" (10:362).

D. ROMAN JAKOBSON

As Professor Emeritus at Harvard and M.I.T., Jakobson merits a category to himself, not only because he is the world's greatest living linguist (which he is), but by virtue of his special relationship to the book. The fact that the *de luxe* edition is dedicated to him removes him from controversies over it, and it is unlikely that he will write about it. He permits me to report, however, that although, not being a Vedist, he feels unqualified to pronounce on Wasson's conclusion, he has been impressed from the first with the caliber of his search. Wasson is free of stereotypes and prejudices that have impeded the Soma quest, his standards of scholarship are of the highest, and he has consistently checked his findings with ranking authorities in every field he has entered.

[I omit the next, long section of my original review, titled "Disputed Points," because it deals with technicalities that are likely to be of interest only to professional Indologists. The issues the experts debate there are: (a) whether evidence outside of India and Iran is relevant for identifying the soma plant; (b) whether the Vedic tropes and epithets for soma refer primarily to the soma plant or to its indwelling god; and (c) soma's relation to urine – whether the startling line in question says that priests piss soma or, metaphorically, that the god Indra does that.]

V. The Book

There remains the book as a physical object, lying open on my desk, inviting comment in its own right as an exhibit in bookmaking.

Wasson's first book, his two-volume opus written with his wife titled *Mushrooms, Russia and History,* appeared in a limited edition of 512 numbered copies. I recall that it rated a multi-paged spread in *Life* magazine, which may help account for the fact that, announced at $125, its sales became so brisk that the surprised publishers started raising the price, and its last copies retailed at twice the original figure. Of *SOMA,* twelve years later, 680 copies were printed of which 250 were allotted to the United States. Being a single volume, its price was kept to $200 (inflation must be kept in mind), and again the stock was exhausted within months.

Is it known what is the most expensive book that has ever been published? Regardless, *SOMA* is by all accounts a sumptuous production. Wasson lavished on the bookmaking dimension of his work the same meticulous attention he devoted to the Soma search itself. The volume is in blue half-leather with a dark blue spine, stamped in gold and slip-covered in fine blue linen cloth. The book was designed by Giovanni Mardersteig and set in Dante type; the text and illustrations were printed by the Stamperia Valdonega, Verona. I have already spoken of the stunning photographs: thirteen color tip-ins of the fly-agaric in its natural habitat. The paper was handmade by Fratelli Magnani, Pescia; pages are of International Size A–4. In all, it is a book lover's dream, and in the three years that have elapsed since its publication it has been hard to come by. In the face of the declining quality in the format of botanical publications in the 1930s, Professor Oakes of Harvard argued that "the results of a scientist's research are jewels worthy of a proper setting." Wasson's book would have satisfied him.

As I was telling the SOMA story in class last fall, noting that to get at the book itself students would have to get the key to the Houghton Rare Book Room at Harvard University, one of them raised his hand to say that he had seen the book in the Tech Coop, M.I.T.'s bookstore, on his way to class. I told him he must have been mistaken, for I felt certain that Wasson's aristocratic tastes precluded a popular edition in principle. Happily, it was I who was mistaken. Popular editions have appeared in both cloth ($15) and paperback ($7.50). They lack the jacket watercolor and generous margins of the original and their paper is not handmade, but in other respects they are faithful to the *de luxe* edition.

VI. Conclusion

Soma seems to have been rediscovered, but why was its identity lost in the first place? Wasson believes that its importance, coupled with the famed mnemonic capacities of the Vedic priests, rules out its having simply been forgotten; it must have been deliberately suppressed. In *SOMA* he proposes, as the reason for suppressing it, distribution problems. As the Aryans moved down the Gangetic plains, this high-altitude mushroom became increasingly more difficult to procure. Inconsistency – now the fly-agaric, now a substitute – proved ecclesiastically unworkable; a patron discovering that rhubarb was used in the sacrifice while his neighbor got the genuine article could be difficult. A crisis developed and the governing Brahmins decided that the originals had to be eliminated completely.

Recently Wasson has been inclining toward a different reason: that the substance may have started to get out of hand. Quality declines in the last *Soma* hymns, and some border on irreverence. Three thousand years in advance of our times, India may have found herself on the brink of a psychedelic mess like the one America created in the 1960s. She wasn't able to close the door on it completely – plenty of *bhang* smoking *sadhus* (wandering ascetics) in whom it is impossible to determine whether *sattva* (illumination) or *tamas* (sloth) predominates, can be found in India right down to the present. But at a critical moment, Wasson hypothesized, the Brahmins did everything they could to prevent such abuse. They would rather have the botanical home of their god forgotten than let him be subjected to profanation. If the hypothesis is correct, it would help to explain why the Buddha felt strongly enough about drugs to list them with murder, theft, lying, and adultery as one of the Five Forbidden Things. It could also throw light on Zarathustra's angry excoriation of those who use inebriating urine in their sacrifices: "When wilt thou do away with the urine of drunkenness with which the priests delude the people" (Avesta, Yasna 48:10).

I will myself stretch this line of thought to its conclusion. Even among those who are religiously responsible, entheogens appear to have (in the parlance of atomic decay) a half-life; their revelations decline. They are also capricious. Opening the gates of heaven at the start, there comes a time – I can attest to this myself – when they begin to open either onto less and less or onto the demonic. It is precisely apposite that the book that introduced the entheogens to the contemporary West, Aldous Huxley's *Doors of Perception,* was followed quickly by his *Heaven and Hell.* It seems that if God can manifest himself through anything, it is equally the case that nothing can commandeer him and guarantee his arrival. It is compatible with the notion that the Absolute entered India by way of a mushroom to hold that sometime later it stopped doing so.

The Sacred Unconscious

Having reached midpoint in this collection of essays, it is time to take stock.

The problem, or rather mystery, that stalks our understanding of the entheogens is how Ultimate Reality or God can disclose him/her/ itself – the pronouns never work – to us through changes in brain chemistry. This chapter addresses that issue head-on. It builds on my essay, "The Sacred Unconscious," which was written for Roger Walsh and Deane Shapiro's book, Beyond Health and Normality: Explorations of Exceptional Psychological Well-Being, but I have reworked that essay substantially to bring it closer to the concerns of this book.

The point of including it reduces to this. In the view of the mind that evolutionary biology, the cognitive sciences, and clinical psychology have assembled, there is no way that entheogenic certainties can be accepted at face value, for the only explanations that that model can offer are ones that explain the certainties away. (I am speaking of course of certainties that retain their force after the conventional world re-forms. Some things that seem certain at the time are easily recognized as nonsense the moment the chemicals wear off. "The entire universe is pervaded by a strong odor of turpentine" is a frequently cited example.) This leaves those who accept those certainties as authentic theophanies needing a different model of the mind to work with.

The model here presented is so at odds with the current model that – fearing that mine will be dismissed out of hand – I will take my cue from football coaches who hold that there are times when the best defense is a good offense. Accordingly, I shall attack.

When it comes to improbabilities, advocates of the current model of the mind are in no position to throw stones. According to this model, the mind is the culmination of a twenty-billion-year history in which – from a mysterious substratum not rightly described as "matter" that the Big

Bang left in its wake – matter evolved from its most elementary constituents into ones that became progressively more complex until organisms appeared. These, in the course of their three-billion-year history on this planet, have developed increasingly ingenious strategies for relating to their environments, with human intelligence the most sophisticated of these.

In its way this is an impressive scenario, but it leaves four things unexplained:

First, how the universe originated in the first place. One of the world's foremost astronomers, Allan Sandage of the Observatories of the Carnegie Institution in Pasadena, California, recently proposed that the Big Bang could only be understood as "a miracle," in which some higher force must have played a role. A fair number of cosmologists are now saying the same.

Second, how, following the Big Bang, matter derived from non-matter. That it did so derive seems now to be accepted, for (as a theoretical physicist at the University of California put it to me recently) if you begin with matter as simply given, you're lost. Yet how quark containment with its rest mass – as serviceable a definition of matter as we have – gets into the picture is something physicists don't like to think about.

Third, how qualities derive from quantities. Even people who recognize the limitations of science assume that it can handle the corporeal world, but it cannot – not in that world's fullness. The world comes to us clothed in sounds and colors and fragrances, which in textbook science have no right to be there, for the electromagnetic waves that underlie those qualities are as close to them as science can get.

Finally, how thoughts and feelings – in short, mind – derive from brain. This fourth difficulty takes us directly to the psychoactive drugs, so it deserves more extended treatment.

To characterize the relation between consciousness and brain activity as "the hard problem" in cognitive science is an understatement, for efforts to understand that connection have failed to a degree unparalleled in any other scientific endeavor. In 1992 a symposium on Experimental and Theoretical Studies of Consciousness was convened by the Ciba

Foundation in London. After three days of deliberations, its participants (all of whom were leading philosophers, neurobiologists, and cognitive scientists) were forced to conclude that the mind-body problem not only remains unsolved; there was not even a consensus on how it might be solved. As one of the participants, Thomas Nagel, put the point, "Unless conscious points of view can be subjected to outright physical reduction [which Nagel doubted they can be], it will not be possible to understand how they necessarily arise in certain kinds of physical systems, described only in terms of contemporary physics and chemistry." Since the Ciba conference, this position has gained strength. Under the ungainly name "mysterianism," it has garnered the support of a number of leading cognitive scientists, including Steven Pinker, head of the Center for Cognitive Science at M.I.T. (See his book How the Mind Works *and Colin McGinn's* The Mysterious Flame.*)*

This impasse that the reigning model of the mind seems to have run into can be taken as an invitation to consider alternatives. That the inspiration for the model that I present here comes from India should not surprise us, given the fact that historically India has been the world's introspective psychologist, having poured roughly as much energy into exploring inner space as the West has devoted to probing the external world.

Dropping several of the opening paragraphs in "The Sacred Unconscious" essay that I wrote for the Walsh/Shapiro volume, I pick up with its discussion of depth psychology.

That a great deal of what goes on in our minds is out of sight is beyond question. Much of our knowledge gets programmed into neural pathways in ways that we neither perceive nor understand in detail. Thus, I rightly say that I know how to ride a bicycle and to type using the touch system, but I am not aware of the workings of this "tacit knowledge," as Michael Polanyi christened it. Atop this physiologically impounded knowledge is the storehouse of memories that can be recalled but are otherwise not in full view. Fragments from this storehouse often arrive uninvited through free associations. Psychologists study the pathways these associations lay down in our early years, and they help us understand ways in which those pathways influence our responses for the rest of our lives. The totality of these pathways constitutes the "individual unconscious" each of us possesses, individual because no childhood duplicates another. To that individual unconscious Marx added a "social unconscious," for our position in the social hierarchy also influences the way we see things. Reading this paragraph backward, we can say that the West has identified three quite well-delineated unconsciouses: a social unconscious (constructed by our place in society), an individual unconscious (which our individual childhood experiences have produced), and a physiological unconscious (which impounds our tacit knowledge).

Learning about these three layers of our unconscious minds has proved useful, but there is a problem. Set within the scientific worldview which sees the mind as having evolved from what lacks mind, they do not provide us with a very inspiring image of ourselves. Artists tend to see this most clearly, and I will quote one of the most discerning among them, Saul Bellow. Speaking of the "contractual daylight" view of ourselves that psychologists, sociologists, historians, and journalists have moved into place, Bellow, in his 1976 Nobel Prize Address, continues:

> The images that come to us in this contractual daylight, so boring to us all, originate in the contemporary worldview. We put into our books the consumer, civil servant, football fan, lover, television viewer. And in the contractual daylight version their life is a kind of death. There is another life, coming from an insistent sense of what we are, that denies these daylight formulations and the false life – the death in life – they make for us. For it is false, and we know it, and our secret and incoherent resistance to it cannot stop, for that resistance arises from persistent intuitions. Perhaps humankind cannot bear too much reality, but neither can it bear too much unreality, too much abuse of truth.

In this context, Roger Walsh and Deane Shapiro's *Beyond Health and Normality: Explorations of Exceptional Psychological Well-Being* comes like a burst of fresh air. As psychiatrists, Walsh and Shapiro are aware of how much Freud contributed to the "boring, contrac-tual daylight" model of the self that Saul Bellow recounts, but they don't stop there. Noting that the complete edition of the collected works of Sigmund Freud contains over four hundred entries for neurosis and none for health, they go on to point out that Freud was a physician and that physicians deal with sick patients. Freud dealt with sick unconsciouses. Walsh and Shapiro ask us in effect to turn this on its head by tying to imagine what a model of the human self might look like if its database numbered saints rather than neurotics.

I shall use the second half of this essay to address that question directly, but because saints constitute a small sample of the human population, I shall begin more neutrally by proposing a model of the human mind that holds for human beings generally and work up from there to the supreme actualization it allows for.

Among other virtues in the paragraph by Saul Bellow that I quoted is its recognition that self-images are shaped by the world-views that prompt them, so I will say in a sentence what it is in the traditional and modern worldviews that causes them to generate opposing anthropological models. Modernity sees humanity as hav-ing ascended from what is inferior to it – life begins in slime and ends in intelligence – whereas traditional cultures see it as de-scended from its superiors. As the anthropologist Marshall Sahlins puts the matter: "We are the only people who assume that we have ascended from apes. Everybody else takes it for granted that they are descended from gods."

I shall be tapping here into the Indian account of this divine lin-eage which traditional peoples universally assumed, and a vivid memory takes me directly to the heart of that account.

In 1970, while conducting thirty students around the world for an academic year to study cultures on location, I availed myself of my professional friendship with a distinguished philosopher at the Uni-versity of Madras, T. M. P. Mahadevan, to ask him to speak to my students. I felt awkward about the invitation for I assigned him an impossible topic, to explain to neophytes in one short morning how Indian philosophy differs from Western philosophy. I needn't have been concerned, for he rose to the occasion effortlessly. Beginning with a sentence that I remember verbatim for the scope it covered, he said, matter-of-factly: "Indian philosophy differs from Western in that Western philosophers philosophize from a single state of consciousness, the waking state, whereas India philosophizes from them all." From that arresting beginning, he went on to explain that India sees waking conscious as one state among four, the other three being the dream state, the state of dreamless sleep, and a final state that is so far from our waking consciousness that it is referred to simply as "the fourth."

I pass over the fact that it is only in the last fifty years that the West has taken serious notice of the difference between dream and dreamless sleep, which difference yogis have worked with for millennia. What is important is not the time scale, but the different ways the two civilizations characterize dreamless sleep. The West does not assume that it includes awareness, whereas India holds that we are then more intensely aware than we are when we are awake or dreaming.

I battled my Vedanta teacher for seven years over that issue, I claiming that I was not aware while sleeping dreamlessly and he insisting that I was aware. When I pointed out that I certainly wasn't *aware* that I was aware, he dismissed my riposte as sophomoric. Think of how rapidly even your dreams evaporate, he said – most of them don't survive until morning. That much I had to grant him, and he went on to press his advantage. Dreamless sleep transpires in a far deeper stratum of the mind than dreams occupy, he said, so it stands to reason that years of (yogic) attention are required to bring its content back to wakeful memory. And what the yogis report is that dreamless sleep is a state of bliss, bliss so intense in fact that it is exceeded only by "the fourth" state of consciousness wherein *atman* (the self's foundation) merges with *Brahman*. Were it not for the fact that we recharge our batteries every twenty-four hours by experiencing this bliss of dreamless sleep, my teacher concluded, the trials and disappointments of daily life would wear us down and we would give up on life.

My swami and I ran out his clock in this deadlock, but several years after he died something happened that brought me around to his position. To have my wisdom teeth extracted I was administered total anesthesia, and in the improbable circumstances of a cramped recovery room with a nurse shaking me to return me to wakefulness, I heard myself exclaiming, "It's so beautiful!" Even as I pronounced those words, my grip on the experience had slipped to the point that I could no longer remember *what* it was that was beautiful, but *that* it was beautiful, staggeringly so, I can remember so vividly that to this day it continues to send chills up my spine. When I reported the incident to one of our daughters, she said that the same thing had happened to her, only her first words were "I love you," professed to a total stranger. "I'm so happy" was the variation a third party reported, while a fourth acquaintance reports that "this is so neat!" was the best his high school vocabulary could manage in describing the experience when it occurred to him.

The question this raises is, what prompted those ecstatic (I use the word advisedly) utterances in their respective modes of beauty, love, and bliss – three faces of God or the Good? (I omit "neat" because of its adolescent vagueness.) Clearly, nothing that was going on in the empirical world. My own conclusion is that all three were reports from the state of "dreamless sleep" that the anesthetics had transported their patients to and whose importance my swami had been trying to persuade me of.

India's model of the mind incorporates these three states of consciousness in a way that positions them (figuratively speaking) as Chinese boxes. *Atman* – the pure, effulgent, undiluted consciousness that is our essence – is encased in what the Indians call the "causal body" which we experience in deep sleep. This in turn nestles in the "subtle body," which fabricates dreams, and that in turn is housed in the "gross body," which generates wakeful experience. As the Pure Light of the Void works its way through these "boxes" – which in Sanskrit are called "sheaths," and which in many traditions are referred to as veils – it grows progressively dimmer and we are brought back to the fundamental difference between the traditional and modern models of the mind that I previously mentioned. Modernity sees the mind as having arisen from what is inferior to it, whereas traditional people see it as deriving from what is greater than itself and carrying within itself traces of its noble ancestry.

Even today we hear echoes of this traditional, less-from-more model of the mind in voices like those of Wordsworth ("trailing clouds of glory we come from heaven, our home"), Eddington (who concluded that the world is more like a mind than a machine), Schrödinger (who likened it to *Brahman:* infinite being, infinite awareness, and infinite bliss), and Bergson (who considered the mind a reducing valve), but I must move on to the second half of this essay. Having called attention to seemingly insuperable problems that plague the modern model of the mind, and following that by dubbing in (in Vedantic idiom) the basics of the generic traditional model, I turn now to the direct object of Walsh and Shapiro's book, which is to explore possibilities of extreme psychological well-being. What kind of person does the traditional model of selfhood allow for at its best?

It is easier to describe flawed instances of the model than perfected ones, for those are the only instances we actually encounter – even Christ asked rhetorically, "Why callest thou me good?" Paradoxically, these tarnished instances are our best resource for trying to imagine a perfected one, as the "tragic flaw" theory of art attests. No playwright would dream of trying to create a perfect hero, for matched with real life he would appear as bogus as a cardboard cutout. But endow the hero with a fatal weakness – Hamlet's indecision is the classic example – and the reader will supply the missing virtue instinctively. Master psychologist that he was, the Buddha anticipated this tragic-flaw device by twenty-five centuries. He never played to the galleries with previews of coming attractions, tantalizing descriptions of what *nirvana* would feel like. What he hammered at was the three poisons that stand in its way: greed, hatred, and delusion. Human egos that result from the veilings of the three sheaths are shot through with these poisons. Interests and thoughts normally extend outward, but our egos work like magnets to bend them back in U-turns onto ourselves. This creates a hot spot of being that hugs us tightly; things that concern us directly we view with feverish intensity, while regarding those at a distance with cold indifference. Our glasses are prescription-ground to cause us to see things our way. It's as the Tibetans say: when a pickpocket meets a saint, what he sees is his pockets. More poignantly, when poor children are asked to draw a penny they draw it larger than do children for whom pennies are commonplace; it looms larger in their minds' eyes. What we take to be objective facts are largely psychological constructs, as the Latin, *factum*, "that which is made," reminds us. The conclusion is inescapable. Our normal self is little more than an amalgam of desires and aversions that we have wound around it as tightly as the elastic of a golf ball.

This tight, constricted, golf-ball self is in for hard knocks, but what concerns me here is that on average it doesn't feel very good. Anxiety hovers over it. It can feel victimized and grow embittered. It is easily disappointed and can become unstrung. To others it often appears no prettier than it feels to itself: petty, self-centered, drab, and bored.

I am deliberately putting down this golf-ball self – hurling it to the ground, as it were, to see how high our total self can bounce: how far toward heaven it can ascend. In order to ascend, it must break out of the hard rubber strings of our attachments that we have stretched so tightly around it. If we change our image from rubber to glass and picture the Three Poisons as a lens that refracts light waves in the direction of our private, importunate demands, freedom from these egocentric distortions will come by, progressively decreasing our lens's curve – reducing its bulge. The logical terminus of this would be clear glass. Through this glass we would be able to see things objectively, as they are in their own right.

This clear glass, which for purposes of vision is equivalent to no glass at all, is our sacred unconscious. It is helpful to think of it as an absence because (like window glass) it functions best when it calls no attention to itself, and it is precisely this absence that makes the world available to us – "the less there is of self, the more there is of Self," as Meister Eckhart said. From clear glass we have moved to no glass – the removal of everything that might separate subject from object, self from world. Zen Buddhists use the image of a Great Round Mirror. When the obscuring deposits of the Three Poisons are removed from it, it reflects the world just as it is.

To claim that human consciousness can move permanently into this condition is (as I have said) probably to go too far, but advances along the asymptotic curve that slopes in its direction are clearly perceptible. When our aversion lens is bloated, humping toward a semicircle, we like very little that comes our way. The same holds, of course, for our desire lens which is only the convex side of aversion's concave arc – the more it distorts our evaluations toward our own self-interests, the less energy remains to appreciate things in their own right. Blake's formulation of the alternative to this self-centered outlook (which I draw upon for the title of this book) has become classic. "If the doors of perception were cleansed, everything would appear to man as it is, infinite."

The fully realized human being is one whose doors of perception have been cleansed – I have myself referred to these doors as windows and envisioned them as successive layers of our unconscious minds.* Those that are near the surface vary from per-

---

* Daniel Brown has uncovered something here that is interesting and perhaps important. Writing in the *International Journal of Clinical and Experimental Hypnosis* (XXV, 4, October 1977), he notes that the steps in Tantric Buddhist meditation reverse the stages of perceptive and cognitive development as these have been discovered by the Constructivist school in child psychology: Piaget, Gesell, Kagan, Lois Murphy, Brunner, *et al*. Paralleling in reverse the processes by which the infant successively acquires (constructs), first a sense of self around which to organize his experience and then structures for organizing his perceptions and after that his thoughts, Tantric meditation dismantles those constructs. After an initial stage that trains the lama to introspect intently, a second state disrupts his thought-structures, regressing him to the world of pure perception. Step three takes over from there and disrupts the perception-patterning processes that moved into place in infancy. The fourth and final stage breaks through the organizing mechanisms that constructed the infant's sense of ego and enables the lama to experience a world in which there is no obstructing sense of self. In the vocabulary of the present essay, such meditation peels back intermediate layers of our unconscious minds and allows us to be in direct touch with our sacred unconscious.

I am indebted to Kendra Smith for the substance of the preceding paragraph and to Jeffrey Becker (a former student of mine who is now a medical student) for calling my attention to this sequel. It appears that direct pharmacological intervention into the brain can produce experiences that may be roughly parallel to those the Tibetans access by meditating, particularly the phenomenon of self-annihilation.

son to person, for they are deposited by our idiosyncratic childhood experiences. At some level, though, we encounter the Three Poisons (once again: desire, aversion, and ignorance) that are common to humankind and to some degree may be necessary for us to function as individuals. But the deepest layer, I have suggested, is really a no-layer, for – being a glass door ajar, or a mirror that discloses other things rather than itself – it effectively isn't there. Even if it were there, in what sense could we call it ours? For when we look toward it we see simply – world.

This opening out onto the world's infinity is one good reason for calling this deepest stratum of the mind sacred, for surely holiness has something to do with the whole. But the concreteness of Blake's formulation is instructive. He doesn't tell us that a cleansed perception discloses the Infinite per se. It finds it in the things at hand, in keeping with the Buddhist teaching that the most sacred scriptures are in unwritten pages – an old pine tree gnarled by wind and weather, or a skein of geese traversing the autumn sky.

Thus far I have defined a realized human being, what the Indians call a *jivamukta*. It remains to describe one. What would it feel like to be such a person, and how would one appear to others?

Basically she lives in the unvarying presence of the numinous. This does not mean that she is excited or "hyped"; her condition has nothing to do with adrenaline flow or manic states that call for depressive ones to balance the emotional account. It's more like what Kipling had in mind when he said of one of his characters, "He believed that all things were one big miracle, and when a man knows that much he knows something to go upon." The opposite of the sense of the sacred is not serenity or sobriety. It is drabness; taken-for-grantedness. Lack of interest. The humdrum and prosaic. The deadly sin of acedia.

The activity of a certain neuronal receptor – the N-methyl-D-aspartate (NMDA) receptor – is particularly essential to the emergence of many higher human processes, including memory and one's sense of self. Blocking the activity of that receptor with nitrous oxide or ketamine can help bring about ego dissolution. Awareness remains, but with ego boundaries lowered or even leveled, the awareness is now experienced as boundless.

All other attributes of a realized being must be relativized against this one absolute: an acute sense of the astonishing mystery of everything. Everything else we say of him must have a yes/no quality. Is he always happy? Well, yes and no. On one level he emphatically is not; if he were, he couldn't "weep with those who mourn" – he would be an unfeeling monster, a callous brute. If anything, a realized soul is *more* in touch with the grief and sorrow that is part and parcel of the human condition, knowing that it too needs to be accepted and lived as all life needs to be lived. To reject the shadow side of life and pass it by with averted eyes, refusing our share of common sorrow while expecting our share of common joy, would cause the unlived, closed-off shadows in us to deepen into fear, including the fear of death.

A story that is told of the recent Zen master Shaku Soen points up the dialectical stance of the realized soul toward the happiness I am noting. In the evening he liked to take a stroll through the outskirts of his village. One evening he heard wailing in a house he was passing, and, on entering quietly, he found that the householder had died and his family and neighbors were crying. Immediately he sat down and started weeping with them. An elderly gentleman, shaken by this display of emotion by an accomplished master, berated him. "I thought you were beyond this kind of thing," he said indignantly. Through his sobs the master managed to falter, "It is this that puts me beyond it."[1]

The master's tears we can understand; the sense in which he was beyond them is more difficult, it being the peace that passeth understanding. The peace that comes when a man is hungry and finds food, is sick and recovers, or is lonely and finds a friend – peace of this sort is comprehensible. But the peace that passeth understanding comes when the pain of life is not relieved. It shimmers on the crest of a wave of pain; it is the spear of frustration transformed into a shaft of light. The master's sobs were real, yet paradoxically they did not erode the yes-experience of the East's "it is as it should be" and the West's "Thy will be done."

In our efforts to conceive the human best, everything turns on an affirmation that steers between cynicism on the one hand and sentimentality on the other. A realized self isn't incessantly and oppressively cheerful – oppressively, not only because we suspect some dissembling in his unvarying smile, but because it underscores our moodiness by contrast. Not every room a *jivamukta* enters floods with light; he can flash anger, and upset money changers' tables. Not invariance but appropriateness is his hallmark, an appropriateness that has the whole repertoire of emotions at its command. The Catholic church is right in linking radiance with sanctity, but the paradoxical, "in spite of" character of this radiance must again be stressed. Along with being a gift to be received, life is a task to be performed. The adept performs it. Whatever her hand finds to do, she does it with a will. Even if it proves her lot to walk stretches of life as a desert waste, she walks it rather than pining for its alternative. Happiness enters as by-product. What matters focally, as the Zen master Dogen never tired of noting, is resolve.

If a *jivamukta* isn't forever radiating sweetness and light, neither does he constantly emit blasts of energy. He can be forceful when need be; we find it restoring rather than draining to be around him, and he has reserves to draw on, as when Socrates stood all night in trance and outpaced the militia with bare feet on ice. In general, though, we sense him as composed rather than charged – the model of the dynamic and magnetic personality tends to have a lot of ego in it for needing to be noticed. Remember: everything save the adept's access to inner vistas, the realms of gold I am calling the sacred unconscious, must be relativized. If leadership is called for, he steps forward; if not, he is pleased to follow. He isn't debarred from being a guru, but he doesn't need disciples to prop up his ego. Focus or periphery, limelight or shadow, it doesn't really matter. Both have their opportunities, both the demands they exact.

All these relativities that I have mentioned – happiness, energy, prominence, impact – pertain to the *jivamukta's* finite self which she progressively pushes aside as she makes her way toward her sacred unconscious. As her goal is an impersonal, impartial one, her identification with it involves a dying to her finite selfhood. Part of her being is engaged in a perpetual vanishing act, as Coomaraswamy suggested when he wrote,

"Blessed is the man on whose tomb can be written, 'Hic jacet nemo,' here lies no one."[2]

But having insisted that there is only one absolute or constant in the journey toward this self-naughting; namely, the sense of the sacred, that luminous mystery in which all things are bathed, I must now concede that there is one other: the realization of how far we all are from the goal that beckons, how many precipices must yet be climbed. As human beings we are created to surpass ourselves and are truly ourselves only when transcending ourselves. Only the slightest of barriers separates us from our sacred unconscious; it is infinitely close to us. But we are infinitely far from it, so for us the barrier looms as a mountain that we must dig through with bare hands. We scrape away at the earth, but in vain; the mountain remains. Still we go on digging at the mountain, in the name of God or whatever.

Of the final truth we for the most part only hear; very rarely do we experience it. The mountain isn't there. It never was there.

This is the one essay in this collection in which entheogens are not mentioned. The reader probably understands why I have included it, but at risk of belaboring the obvious I will be explicit. In ways (and for reasons that no one understands) entheogens hold the possibility of opening the doors of perception to the sacred unconscious.

Contemporary Evidence:
Psychiatry and the Work of Stanislav Grof

In 1976 I published a book, Forgotten Truth: The Primordial Tradition, which sketched in broad outlines the worldview, and correlative model of the human self, to which all traditional societies subscribed.

Shortly before completing that book, I came upon the groundbreaking work of a Czech psychiatrist, Dr. Stanislav Grof, who had researched the entheogens more systematically than any other scientist. In Czechoslovakia he was assigned to determine whether LSD is a potential cure for schizophrenia. Child of his time and in the Soviet orbit – the Iron Curtain was solidly in place then – he had been schooled on the mechanistic, Pavlovian model of the mind which his psychiatric professors claimed was scientific. His own psychoanalysis, together with what came to light in the seventeen years (and more than twelve thousand clinical hours) he spent researching LSD with his patients, convinced him of the opposite.

I found his findings so in keeping with the traditional concept of the self that I had outlined in my book that I added an Appendix to my book to summarize his work. This chapter reprints that Appendix. It relates to the present book as follows: Whereas the preceding chapter proposed a model of the human self that allows room for authentic entheogenic revelations, this one doubles back on that chapter to use the entheogens to validate that model itself.

To tie those two essays together, I have included here the Sanskrit terms that I employed in the preceding chapter but which are not in the original version of this essay. In the interests of smoother reading I have deleted the footnotes that show where the statements by Grof that I quote verbatim appear in his corpus. Those who want that information can find it in the Appendix of Forgotten Truth (HarperSanFrancisco, 1976, 1994).

Know ten things, tell nine, the Taoists say – one wonders whether it is wise even to mention the entheogens in connection with God and the Infinite. For though a connection exists, as is the case with sex in Tantra, it is next to impossible to speak of it in the West today without being misunderstood. Such potential misunderstanding may be the reason that the identity of the Eleusinian sacrament is one of history's best-kept secrets, and why Brahmins came eventually to conceal (and then deliberately forget) the identity of Soma.

If the only thing to say about the entheogens were that they seem on occasion to disclose higher planes of consciousness and perhaps the Infinite itself, I would hold my peace. For though such experiences may be veridical in ways, the goal (it cannot be stressed too often) is not religious experiences, but the religious life. And with respect to the latter, chemically occasioned "theophanies" can abort a quest as readily as they can further it.

It is not, therefore, the isolated mystical experiences that entheogens can occasion that leads me to add this Appendix to *Forgotten Truth*, but rather evidence of a different order. Long-term, professionally garnered, and carefully weighed, this second kind of evidence deserves to be called (if anything in this murky area merits the attribution) scientific. I report that evidence here because of the ways in which (and extent to which) it seems to corroborate the primordial anthropology that *Forgotten Truth* presents and my preceding chapter summarizes. In contradistinction to writings on the entheogens that are occupied with experiences the mind can *have,* my concern here is with evidence they afford as to what the mind *is.*

The evidence in question is not widely known, for it has been reported only in a few relatively obscure journals and a single book. Still, judged both by the caliber of the data encompassed and the explanatory power of the hypotheses that make sense of the data, it is the most impressive evidence that the entheogens have thus far produced. It came together through the work of Stanislav Grof.

Grof's work began in Czechoslovakia, where for four years he worked in an interdisciplinary complex of research institutes in

Prague, and for another seven in the Psychiatric Research Institute in the same city. On coming to the United States in 1967 he continued his investigations at the Research Unit of Spring Grove State Hospital in Baltimore. Two covering facts about his work are worth noting before I turn to its content. First, in the use of LSD for therapy and personality assessment, his experience is by far the vastest that any single individual has amassed, covering as it does over twenty-five hundred sessions in each of which he spent a minimum of five hours with its subject. In addition, his studies cover another eight hundred cases that his colleagues in Prague and Baltimore conducted. Second, in spanning the Atlantic his work straddles the two dominant approaches to LSD therapy that have been developed: psycholytic therapy (used at Prague and favored in Europe generally), which involves numerous administrations of low-to-medium doses of LSD or its variants over a long therapeutic program, and high-dose therapy (confined to America), which involves one or several high-dose sessions in a short period of treatment.

The first thing Grof and his associates discovered was that there is no specific pharmacological effect that LSD invariably produces: "I have not been able to find a single phenomenon that could be considered an invariant product of the chemical action of the drug in any of the areas studied – perceptual, emotional, ideational, and physical." Not even mydriasis (prolonged dilation of the pupils), one of the most common symptoms, occurs invariably. Psychological effects vary even more than do physiological, but the range of the latter – mydriasis, nausea and vomiting, enhanced intestinal movements, diarrhea, constipation, frequent urination, acceleration as well as retardation of pulse, cardiac distress and pain, palpitations, suffocation and dyspnea, excessive sweating and hypersalivation, dry mouth, reddening of the skin, hot flushes and chills, instability and vertigo, inner trembling, fine muscle tremors – exceeds that of any other drug that affects the autonomic nervous system. These somatic symptoms are practically independent of dosage and ·occur in all possible combinations. Variability between subjects is equaled by variation in the symptoms a single subject will experience under different circumstances; particularly important from the clinical point of view are the differences that appear at different stages in the therapeutic process. All of this led Grof to conclude that LSD is not a specific causal agent, but rather a catalyst. It is an unspecific amplifier of neural and mental processes. By exteriorizing for the therapist, and raising to consciousness for the patient himself, material that is otherwise buried, and by enlarging this material to the point of caricature so that it appears as if under a magnifying glass, the LSD-like drugs are (Grof became convinced) unrivaled instruments: first, for identifying causes in psychopathology (the problem that is causing the difficulty); second, for personality diagnosis (determining the character type of the subject in question); and third, for understanding the human mind generally. "It does not seem inappropriate to compare their potential significance for psychiatry and psychology to that of the microscope for medicine or of the telescope in astronomy. Freud called dreams the 'royal way to the unconscious.' The statement is valid to a greater extent for LSD experiences."

Of the drug's three potentials, it is the third – its resources for enlarging our understanding of the human mind and self – that concerns us in this book. The nature of man is so central to our study that even flickers of light from Grof's work would make it interesting. That the light proves to be remarkably clear and steady makes it important.

Let me move at once to the point. The traditional view of human beings presents them as multilayered creatures, and Grof's work points to that same conclusion. As long as the matter is put thus generally it signals nothing novel, for standard depth psychology – psychiatry and psychoanalysis – concurs: the adjective "depth" implies as much, and metaphors of archaeology and excavation lace the writings of Freud, Jung, and their ilk. The novelty of Grof's work lies in the precision with which the levels of the mind that it uncovers correspond with the levels of selfhood the primordial tradition postulates.

In chemo-excavation the levels come to view sequentially. In this respect, too, images of archaeology apply: surface levels must be uncovered to get at ones that lie deeper. In high-dose therapy the deeper levels tend to appear later in the course of a single session; in psycholytic (low-dose) therapy they usually surface later in the sequence of therapeutic sessions. The sequences are the same, but since the levels first came to Grof's attention during his psycholytic work in Prague, and since that earlier work was the more extensive – it spanned eleven of the seventeen years he worked with the drugs – I shall confine myself to it in reporting his experimental work.

The basic study at Prague included fifty-two psychiatric patients. All major clinical categories were represented, from depressive disorders through psychoneuroses, psychosomatic diseases, and character disorders to borderline and clear-cut psychoses in the schizophrenic group. Patients with above-average intelligence were favored to obtain high-quality introspective reports; otherwise, cases with dim prognosis in each category were chosen. Grof himself worked with twenty-two of the subjects, his two colleagues with the remainder. The number of psycholytic sessions ranged from fifteen to one hundred per patient with a total of over twenty-five hundred sessions being conducted. Each patient's treatment began with several weeks of drug-free psychotherapy. Thereafter the therapy was punctuated with doses of 100 to 250 micrograms of LSD administered at seven- to fourteen-day intervals.

The basic finding was that "when material from consecutive LSD sessions of the same person was compared it became evident that there was a definite continuity between these sessions. Rather than being unrelated and random, the material seemed to represent a successive unfolding of deeper and deeper levels of the unconscious with a very definite trend."

The trend regularly led through three successive stages preceded by another which, being less important psychologically, Grof calls a preliminary phase. In this opening phase the chemical works primarily on the subject's body. In this respect it resembles what earlier researchers had called the vegetative phase, but the two are not identical. Proponents of a vegetative phase assumed that LSD directly causes the manifold somatic responses that patients typically experience in the early stages of the sessions. I have already mentioned that Grof's more extensive evidence counters this view. Vegetative symptoms are real enough, but they vary so much between subjects (and for a single subject under varying circumstances) that it seems probable that they are occasioned more by anxieties and resistances than by the chemical's direct action. There is also the fact that they are far from confined to early phases of the LSD sequence. These considerations led Grof to doubt that there is a vegetative phase per se. The most he is prepared to admit is that the drug has a tendency at the start to affect one specific part of the body: its perceptual and particularly its optical apparatus. Colors become exceptionally bright and beautiful, objects and persons are geometrized, things vibrate and undulate, one hears music as if one were somehow inside it, and so on. This is as close as the drug comes to producing a direct somatic effect, but that effect suffices to warrant speaking of an introductory phase which Grof calls "aesthetic."

With this preliminary phase behind him, the subject begins his psycholytic journey proper. Its first stage is occupied with material that is psychodynamic in the standard sense: Grof calls it the psychodynamic or Freudian stage. Experiences here are of a distinctly personal character. They involve regression into childhood and the reliving of traumatic infantile experiences in which Oedipal and Electra conflicts and ones relating to various libidinal zones are conspicuous; first and last, pretty much the full Freudian topography is traversed. The amount of unfinished business this layer of the self contains varies enormously; as would be expected, in disturbed subjects there is more than in normal ones. But the layer itself is present in everyone and must be worked through before the next stratum can be reached. "Worked through" again means essentially what psychiatry stipulates: a reliving not only in memory but also in emotion of the traumatic episodes that have unconsciously crippled the patient's responses. Freud and Breuer's hypothesis – that insufficient emotional and motor abreaction during early traumatic episodes produces a "jamming" of affect that provides energy for ensuing neurotic symptoms – is corroborated, for when patients in the course of a number of sessions enter into a problem area to the point of reliving it completely and integrating it into consciousness, the symptoms related to that area "never reappear" and the patient is freed to work on other symptoms.

This much was in keeping with Grof's psychiatric orientation; it came as "laboratory proof of the basic premises of psychoanalysis." But there that model gave out. For the experiences that followed, "no adequate explanation can be found within the framework of classical Freudian psychoanalysis."

Negatively, the new stage was characterized by an absence of the individual, biographically determined material that had dominated the sessions theretofore. As a result, the experiential content of this second stage was more uniform for the population than was the content of the first. I have already cited Grof's contention that LSD is not so much an agent that produces specific effects as it is an amplifier of material that is already present, and in the first stage the enlarging process worked to magnify individual differences: "The sessions of patients belonging to various diagnostic categories were characterized by an unusual inter- and also intra-individual variability." In the second stage the results reversed. With the magnifying glass still in place, variations receded: "The content seemed to be strikingly similar in all of the subjects." This is already important, for the emergent similarity suggests that the subjects were entering a region of the mind which they shared in common, a region that underlay the differing scrawls their separate biographies had incised upon it. As to content, "the central focus and basic characteristics of the experience on this level are the problems related to physical pain and agony, dying and death, biological birth, aging, disease and decrepitude" – the Buddha's First Noble Truth, Grof somewhere observes, and the three of the Four Passing Sights that informed it. Inevitably, he continues,

> the shattering encounter with these critical aspects of human existence and the deep realization of the frailty and impermanence of man as a biological creature is accompanied by an agonizing existential crisis. The individual comes to realize through these experiences that no matter what he does in his

85

life, he cannot escape the inevitable: he will have to leave this world bereft of everything that he has accumulated, achieved and has been emotionally attached to.

Among the phenomena of this second stage, the theme of death and rebirth recurred so frequently that it sent Grof to a book he had heard of in his psychiatric training but had not read, it having been written by a psychoanalytic renegade, Otto Rank. It bore the title *The Trauma of Birth*, and, to use Grof's own word, he was "flabbergasted" to find how closely second-stage psycholytic experiences conformed to it. He and his colleagues fell to calling the second stage perinatal or Rankian.

During the weeks through which this stage extends, the patient's clinical condition often worsens. The stage climaxes in a session in which the patient experiences the agony of dying and appears – to himself – actually to die.

> The subjects can spend hours in agonizing pain, with facial contortions, gasping for breath and discharging enormous amounts of muscular tension in various tremors, twitching, violent shaking and complex twisting movements. The color of the face can be dark purple or dead pale, and the pulse rate considerably accelerated. The body temperature usually oscillates in a wide range, sweating can be profuse, and nausea with projectile vomiting is a frequent occurrence.

This death experience tends to be followed immediately by rebirth, an explosive ecstasy in which joy, freedom, and the promise of life of a new order are the dominant motifs.

Outside the LSD sequence, the new life showed itself in the patients' marked clinical improvement. Within the sequence it introduced a third experiential landscape. When Grof's eyes became acclimated to it, it appeared at first to be Jungian, Jung being the only major psychologist to have dealt seriously and relatively unreductively with the visions that appear. Later it seemed better to refer to the stage as "transpersonal."

Two features defined this third and final stage. First, its "most typical characteristics . . . were profound religious and mystical experiences."

Everyone who experientially reached these levels developed convincing insights into the utmost relevance of spiritual and religious dimensions in the universal scheme of things. Even the most hardcore materialists, positivistically oriented scientists, skeptics and cynics, uncompromising atheists and anti-religious crusaders such as the Marxist philosophers, became suddenly interested in spiritual search after they confronted these levels in themselves.

Grof speaks of levels in the plural here, for the "agonizing existential crisis" of the second stage is already religious in its way – death and rebirth are ultimates or there are none. The distinguishing feature of the third stage is not, strictly speaking, that it is religious, but that it is (as Grof's works indicate) mystically religious: religious in a mode in which (a) the whole subsumes its parts, and (b) evil is thereby rescinded. This connects with the stage's other feature, its transpersonal aspect, which was so pronounced as to present itself in the end as the best name for that stage. A trend toward transpersonal experiences, in which one is occupied with things other than oneself, had already shown itself in stage two. Suffering, for example, which in the first stage presented itself in the form of recollected autobiographical traumas, had in the second stage taken the form of identifying with the suffering of others, usually groups of others: famine victims, prisoners in concentration camps, or humankind as a whole with its suffering as symbolized by Christ on his cross, Tantalus exposed to eternal tortures in Hades, Sisyphus sentenced to roll a boulder uphill incessantly, Ixion fixed on the wheel, or Prometheus chained to his rock. Likewise with death. Already by stage two "the subjects felt that they were operating in a framework which was 'beyond individual death.'" The third stage continues this outbound, transpersonal momentum. Now the phenomena with which the subject identifies are not restricted to humankind or even to living forms. They are cosmic, having to do with the elements and forces from which life proceeds. And the subject is less conscious of himself as separate from what he perceives. To a large extent the subject-object dichotomy itself disappears.

So much for description of the three stages. Now to interpretation and explanation.

Grof was and is a psychiatrist. Psychiatry is the study and practice of ontogenetic explanations: it accounts for present syndromes in terms of its patients' antecedent experiences. Freud had mined these experiences as they occur in infancy and childhood, but Grof's work had led to regions that Freud's map did not reveal. As a psychiatrist, Grof had nowhere to turn for explanations save further in the same direction – further back. His methodology forced him to take seriously the possibility that experiences attending birth and even gestation could affect ensuing life trajectories.

Taking his cues from *The Trauma of Birth* while amending it in important respects, Grof worked out a typology in which second- and third-stage LSD experiences are correlated with four distinct stages in the birth process: (a) a comfortable, intrauterine stage before the onset of labor; (b) an oppressive stage at labor's start when the fetus suffers the womb's contractions and has "no exit" because the cervix has not opened; (c) the traumatic ensuing stage of labor during which the fetus is violently ejected through the birth canal; and (d) the freedom and release of birth itself. Stages (b) and (c) seemed to Grof to vector the second or Rankian stage in the LSD sequence. In the reliving of (b), the oppressiveness of the womb is generalized, causing the entire world and existence itself to seem oppressive; and when (c) – the agony of labor and forced expulsion through the birth canal – is relived, this produces the experience of dying: traumatic ejection from the only life-giving context the fetus has known. The rebirth experience (in which the Rankian stage climaxes) derives from reliving the experience of physical birth (d) and paves the way for the ensuing transpersonal stage. The sense of unshadowed bliss that dominates this final stage plugs into the earliest memories of all, those that precede the time when the womb was congested, back when the fetus was blended with its mother in mystic embrace (a). Some cognitive scientists reject this aspect of Grof's work on grounds that the brain structures known to support memory do not develop until months after birth, but Grof replies that this assumes a specificity regarding the neural underpinnings of memory in its entirety that has not been proven. When subjects in their Rankian stage report first suffocation and then a violent, projective explosion in which not only blood but urine and feces are everywhere, one is persuaded that revived memories of the birth process play some part in triggering, shaping, and energizing later-stage LSD experiences. The question is: Are they the only causes at work? As I have noted, in the psychiatric model of humankind, once the Freudian domain has been exhausted there is nowhere to look for causes save where Rank did, and where Grof followed him in looking. Driven back to earlier and yet earlier libido positions, the ego finally reenters the uterus.

In the anthropological model that *Forgotten Truth* and the preceding chapter of the present book describe, things are different. Therein, the social and biological histories of the organism are not the sole resources for explanation. "The soul that rises with us, / Hath had elsewhere its setting, / And cometh from afar: / Not in entire forgetfulness . . . / But trailing clouds of glory do we come." If we ask from whence we come, Wordsworth answers, "from God" and traditional people in principle agree. More proximately, however, it is from the psychic plane – our subtle bodies or souls – that our gross bodies derive. In the psychiatric perspective, bodies are basic, and explanations for mental occurrences are sought in the body's endowments and history, whereas in the traditional model physical bodies represent a kind of shaking out of mental phenomena that precede and are more real than their physical printouts.

Thus, to Grof's finding that later stages in the LSD sequence conform sufficiently to the stages of the birth process to warrant our saying that they are influenced by those stages, tradition adds: "influenced by" only, not caused by. The experiences of those stages put the subject in direct touch with the psychic and archetypal forces of which his life is a distillation and product. For birth and death are not physical only. This much everyone knows, but it is less recognized that physical birth and death are relatively minor manifestations of forces that are cosmic in blanketing the manifest world. Buddhism's *pratitya-samutpada* (Formulation of

Dependent Origination) speaks profoundly to this point, but all I shall say is that when a psychic quantum, the germ of an ego, decides – out of ignorance, the Buddhists insert immediately – that it would be interesting to go it alone and have an independent career, in separating itself from the whole (and in ways setting itself against the whole) the ego shoulders consequences. Because it is finite, things will not always go its way: hence suffering. And the temporal side of the self's finitude ordains that it will die – incrementally from the start as cells and early ambitions die, and eventually in its entirety. Energy is indestructible, however, so in some form there is rebirth. Confrontation of these principal truths in their transpersonal and trans-species generality is the stuff of the later-stage LSD experience. Biological memory enters, but conceivably with little more than a "me too": I too (that memory insists) know the sequence from the time when I was formed and delivered.

Spelled out in greater detail, the primordial explanation of the sequence runs as follows. Accepting LSD as a "tool for the study of the structure of human personality; of its various facets and levels," we see it uncovering the successively deeper layers of the self which Grof's study brings to light. Grof's psychiatric explanation for why it does so is that "defense systems are considerably loosened, resistances decrease, and memory recall is facilitated to a great degree. Deep unconscious material emerges into consciousness and is experienced in a complex symbolic way." The traditional explanation shifts the emphasis. Only in the first stage are the loosened defense systems ones that the individual ego has built to screen out painful memories. For the rest, what is loosened are structures that condition the human mode of existence and separate it from modes that are higher: its corporeality and compliance with the spatio-temporal strictures the gross body must conform to. The same holds for the memory-recall that LSD facilitates. In the first stage it is indeed recollections of experiences that are activated as the subject relives, directly or in symbolic guise, the things the subject individually experienced that are brought to light. But as the archeology delves deeper, what the psychiatrist continues to class as individual recollections – an even earlier, intrauterine memory – the ontologist (short of invoking reincarnation) sees as the discovery of layers of selfhood that are present from conception but are normally obscured from view. Likewise with the "peculiar double orientation and double role of the subject" that Grof describes. "On the one hand," he writes, the subject "experiences full and complex age regression into the traumatic situations of childhood; on the other hand, he can assume alternately or even simultaneously the position corresponding to his real age." This oscillation characterizes the entire sequence, but only in the first stage is its not-immediate referent the past. In the later sessions, that which is not immediate is removed not in time but in space – psychological space, of course. It lies below the surface of the exterior self that is normally in view.

The paradigm of the self that is sketched in chapter 4 of *Forgotten Truth* and the preceding chapter in the book in hand shows it to have four components: body, mind, soul, and Spirit; in the nomenclature of this book, gross body, subtle body, causal body, and "the Fourth." Working with spatial imagery, we can liken LSD to an MRI scan that sweeps progressively toward the core of the subject's being. In the early sessions of the LSD sequence it moves through the subject's body in two steps. The first of these triggers peripheral somatic responses (most regularly ones relating to perception) to produce the aesthetic phase. The second moves into memory regions of the brain where traces of past experiences are stored. That the events that were most important in the subject's formation are the ones that rush forward for attention, stands to reason. We are into the first of the three main stages of the psycholytic sequence, the psychodynamic or Freudian stage.

Passage from the Freudian to the Rankian stage occurs when the chemicals enter the region of the mind that outdistances the brain and swims in the psychic plane which is the subtle body's medium. The phenomenological consequences could almost have been predicted:

1. Biographical data – which imprinted themselves on the subject's body, specifically the memory region of his brain – recede.

2. Their place is taken by "existentials," the conditioning structures of human existence in general. The grim affect of this stage could be due in part to memories of the ordeals of gestation and birth; but the torment – the anguish arising from the realization of the amount of suffering that is endemic to life – derives mainly from the fact that the larger purview of the intermediate plane renders the inherent contractions of the terrestrial plane (*dukkha*) more visible than when the subject is individually immersed in them.

3. In the death-and-rebirth experience that climaxes this phase, Rankian considerations could play a part while again not preempting the show. The self had entered the psychic plane through the causal body's assumption of – compression into – the subtle body's sheath. Now, in reversing this sequence, the subtle body must die in order to return to its more august causal body.

Descriptions of this return appear regularly in subjects' reports of the transpersonal stage in their treatment. Here are some of its features:

1. Whereas in the Rankian stage "there was a very distinct polarity between very positive and very negative experience," experience is now predominantly beatific, with "melted ecstasy" perhaps its most-reported theme. Subjects "speak about mystic union, the fusion of the subjective with the objective world, identification with the universe, cosmic consciousness, the intuitive insight into the essence of being, the Buddhist's *nirvana*, the Veda's *samadhi*, the harmony of worlds and spheres, the approximation to God, etc."

2. Experience is more abstract. At its peak it "is usually contentless and accompanied by visions of blinding light or beautiful colors (heavenly blue, gold, the rainbow spectrum, peacock feathers, etc.)" or is associated with space or sound. When its accoutrements are more concrete they tend to be archetypal, with the archetypes seeming to be limitless in number.

3. The God who is almost invariably encountered is single and so far removed from anthropomorphism as to elicit, often, the

pronoun "it." This is in contrast to the gods of the Rankian stage who tend to be multiple, Olympian, and essentially human beings writ large.

4. Beyond the causal body (soul) lies only "the Fourth," (Spirit), an essence so ineffable that when the seeing eye perceives it, virtually all that can be reported is that it is "beyond" and "more than" all that had been encountered theretofore.

The correlations between traditional anthropology and the LSD sequence can be diagrammed as follows.

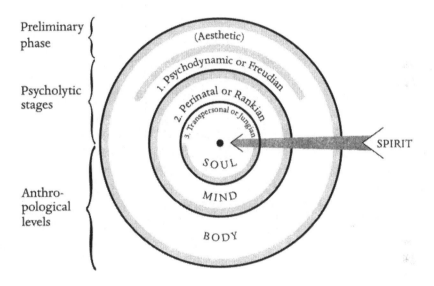

Up to this point I have summarized Grof's empirical findings and pointed to how they can be explained by the traditional model of the human self as readily as by his psychiatric model. It remains to note how the findings of his seventeen years of research affected his own thinking.

Engaged as he was in "the first mapping of completely unknown territories," he could not have foreseen where his inquiry would lead. What he found was that in "the most fascinating intellectual and spiritual adventure of my life, it opened up new fantastic areas and forced me to break with the old systems and frameworks."

The first change in his thinking has already been noted: the psycholytic sequences showed the birth trauma to have more dynamic consequences than Grof and his strictly Freudian associates had supposed. This change psychoanalysis could accommodate, but not the one that followed. "I started my LSD research in 1956 as a convinced and dedicated psychoanalyst," he writes. "In the light of everyday clinical observations in LSD sessions, I found this conception untenable." Basically, what proved to be untenable was "the present gloomy image of man, which is to a great extent influenced by psychoanalysis."[1] This picture of man,

> that of a social animal basically governed by blind and irrational instinctual forces, contradicts the experiences from the LSD sessions, or at least appears in their light superficial and limited. Most of the instinctual tendencies described by psychoanalysis (incestuous and murderous wishes, cannibalistic impulses, sadomasochistic inclinations, coprophilia, etc.) are very striking in the early LSD sessions; they are so common that they could almost be considered experimental evidence for some of the basic assumptions of psychoanalysis. Most of them, however, appear in the sessions for only a limited period of time. This whole area can be transcended, whereupon we are confronted with an image of man that is diametrically opposed to the previous one. Man in his innermost nature appears then as a being that is fundamentally in harmony with his environment and is governed by intrinsically high and universal values.

This change in anthropology has been the solid effect of entheogenic evidence on Grof's thinking. In psychoanalytic terms, Freud discovered the importance of infantile experience on ontogenetic development, Rank the importance of the experience of birth itself, and Grof's discoveries carry this search for ever earlier etiologies – in psychoanalytic theory earlier means stronger – to its logical limit: his optimistic view of man derives from discovering the influence and latent power of early-gestation memories of the way things were when the womb was still uncongested and all was well.

Beyond this revised anthropology, however, Grof has toyed with a changed ontology as well. Endowments that supplement his psychiatric competences have helped him here: he has a "musical ear," so to speak, for metaphysics, and an abiding interest in the subject. These caused him to listen attentively from the start to his subjects' reports on the nature of reality, and in one of his recent papers, "LSD and the Cosmic Game: Outline of Psychedelic Cosmology and Ontology," he gives these reports full rein. Laying aside for the interval his role as research psychiatrist, which required his seeing his patients' experiences as shaped by (if not projected from) early formative experiences, in this paper Grof turns phenomenologist and allows their reports to stand in their own right. The view of reality that results is so uncannily like the traditional one that *Forgotten Truth* and the preceding chapter of this book outline that, interweaving direct quotations from Grof's article (without bothering with quotation marks) with ones from those two sources, the picture that emerges looks like this:

The ultimate source of existence is the Void, the supracosmic Silence, the uncreated and absolutely ineffable Supreme.

The first possible formulation of this source is Universal Mind. Here, too, words fail, for Universal Mind transcends the dichotomies, polarities, and paradoxes that harass the relative world and our finite minds' comprehension of it. Insofar as description is attempted, the Vedantic ternary – Infinite Existence, Infinite Intelligence, Infinite Bliss – is as serviceable as any.

God is not limited to his foregoing, "abstract" modes. He can be encountered concretely, as the God of the Old and New Testaments, Buddha, Shiva, or in other modes. These modes do not, however, wear the mantle of ultimacy or provide final answers.

The phenomenal worlds owe their existence to Universal Mind, which Mind does not itself become implicated in their categories. Man, together with the three-dimensional world he experiences, is but one of innumerable modes through which Mind experiences itself. The heavy physicality and seemingly objective finality of man's material world, its space-time grid and the laws of nature that offer themselves as if they were the *sine qua nons* of existence itself – all these are in fact highly provisional and relative. Under exceptional circumstances, people can rise to a level of consciousness at which they see that taken together they constitute but one of innumerable sets of limiting constructs that Universal Mind assumes. To saddle that Mind itself with those constructs would be as ridiculous as trying to understand the human mind through the rules of chess.

Created entities tend progressively to lose contact with their original source and the awareness of their pristine identity with it. In the initial stage of this falling away, those entities maintain contact with their source, and the separation is playful, relative, and obviously tentative. An image that illustrates this stage is that of a wave of the ocean. From a certain point of view the wave is a distinct entity – we can speak of it as large, fast-moving, green, and foamy. But its individuation doesn't keep it from belonging to the ocean proper.

At the next stage, created entities assume a partial independence and we can observe the beginnings of cosmic screenwork, the Absolute's assumption of veils that are gossamer-like in the beginning but grow increasingly opaque. Here unity with the source can be temporarily forgotten in the way an actor can forget his own identity as he identifies with the character he depicts.

Eventually the veiling process reaches a point where individuation looks like the normal state of things and the original wholeness is perceived only intuitively and sporadically. This can be likened to the relationship between cells of a body and the body as a whole. Cells are separate entities but function as their body's parts. Individuation and participation are dialectically combined. Complex biochemical interactions bridge provisional boundaries to ensure the functioning of the organism as a whole.

In the final stage, the separation is practically complete. Liaison with the source is lost sight of and the original identity forgotten. The screen is now all but impermeable, and a radical change of consciousness is required to break through it. A snowflake can serve as a symbol. In outward appearance it doesn't look like water; to understand that nevertheless it is water we have to get down to H_2O.

Human beings who manage to effect the requisite breakthrough find thereafter that life's polarities paradoxically do and do not exist. This holds for such contraries as matter and spirit, good and evil, permanence and change, heaven and hell, beauty and ugliness, and agony and ecstasy. In the end, there is no difference between subject and object, observer and observed, experiencer and experienced, creator and creation.

In the early years of psychoanalysis when hostility was shown to its theories on account of their astonishing novelty and they were dismissed as products of their authors' perverted imaginations, Freud used to hold up against this objection the argument that no human brain could have invented such facts and connections had they not been persistently forced on it by a series of converging and interlocking observations. Grof might argue in the same way: to wit, that the cosmology and ontology that his patients came up with is as uninventable as Freud's own system. Actually, however, he does not do so. In the manner of a good phenomenologist, he lets the evidence speak for itself, neither undermining it by referring it back to causes which (in purporting to explain it) would explain it away nor arguing that it is true. As phenomenologists themselves would say, he "brackets" his own judgment regarding the truth question and contents himself with summarizing what his patients said.

The idea that the "three-dimensional world" is only one of many experiential worlds created by the Universal Mind appeared to them much more logical than the opposite alternative that is so frequently taken for granted, namely, that the material world has objective reality of its own and that the human consciousness and the concept of God are merely products of highly organized matter, the human brain. When closely analyzed the latter concept presents at least as many incongruities, paradoxes and absurdities as the concept of the Universal Mind. Problems such as the finitude versus infinity of time and space; the enigma of the origin of matter, energy and space; and the mystery of the prime impulse appear to be so overwhelming and defeating that one seriously questions why this approach should be given priority in our thinking.

The Good Friday Experiment

Mention *has already been made of the Good Friday Experiment, in which – to test the power of entheogens to occasion mystical experiences in a religious setting – Walter Pahnke conducted a study in which theological professors and students were, in 1962, given psilocybin preceding the traditional Good Friday service at Boston University. The project was the research topic for the doctoral degree he received from Harvard University.*

In addition to the detailed report of the experiment that appeared in Pahnke's doctoral dissertation, there have been a number of journalistic accounts of it and a study of the long-term consequences of that day for its subjects (see references at the back of this book). However, one significant incident that occurred during the experiment had not appeared in the reports, and as I was party to it, Thomas Roberts, Professor of Educational Psychology at Northern Illinois University, interviewed me about it to read it into the record. Robert Jesse of the Council on Spiritual Practices was in attendance.

THOMAS ROBERTS

This is October First, 1996. Huston Smith will be telling us about an event that happened in the Good Friday Experiment in 1962. Huston, do you want to tell us about the student who ran out on the experiment?

HUSTON SMITH

Just keep me on course.

ROBERTS

O.K.

SMITH

The basic facts of the experiment have been recorded elsewhere and are fairly well known, but I will summarize them briefly. In the early sixties, Walter Pahnke, a medical doctor with strong interests in mysticism, wanted to augment his medical knowledge with a doctorate in religion. He had heard that the entheogens often occasion mystical experiences, so he decided to make that issue the subject of his research. He obtained the support of Howard Thurman, Dean of Marsh Chapel at Boston University, for his project, and also that of Walter Houston Clark who taught psychology of religion at Andover Newton Theological Seminary and shared Wally's interest in the entheogens.

Clark procured twenty volunteer subjects, mostly students from his seminary. Ten more volunteers, of whom I was one, were recruited as guides. Howard Thurman's two-and-a-half-hour 1962 Good Friday service at Boston University would be piped down to a small chapel in the basement of the building where the volunteers would participate in it. Fifteen of us would receive, double blind, a dose of psilocybin, and the remaining fifteen a placebo: nicotinic acid, which produces a tingling sensation that could make its recipients think they had gotten the real thing. The day after the experiment we would write reports of our experiences, and Pahnke would have them scored by independent raters on a scale of from zero to three for the degree to which each subject's experience included the seven traits of mystical experience that W. T. Stace lists in his classic study, *Mysticism and Philosophy*. There was one borderline case, but apart from that, the experiences of those who received psilocybin were dramatically more mystical than those in the control group. I was one of those who received the psilocybin, and I will say a word about my experience before I proceed to the student that you asked about.

The experiment was powerful for me, and it left a permanent mark on my experienced worldview. (I say "experienced worldview" to distinguish it from what I think and believe the world is like.) For as long as I can remember I have believed in God, and I have experienced his presence both within the world and when the world was transcendentally eclipsed. But until the Good Friday Experiment, I had had no direct personal encounter with God of the sort that *bhakti yogis*, Pentecostals, and born-again Christians describe. The Good Friday Experiment changed that, presumably because the service focused on God as incarnate in Christ.

For me, the climax of the service came during a solo that was sung by a soprano whose voice (as it came to me through the prism of psilocybin) I can only describe as angelic. What she sang was no more than a simple hymn, but it entered my soul so deeply that its opening and closing verses have stayed with me ever since.

> *My times are in Thy hands, my God, I wish them there;*
> *My life, my friends, my soul, I leave entirely in Thy care. . . .*
>
> *My times are in Thy hands, I'll always trust in Thee;*
> *And after death at Thy right hand I shall forever be.*

In broad daylight those lines are not at all remarkable, but in the context of the experiment they said everything. The last three measures of each stanza ascended to a dominant seventh which the concluding tonic chord then resolved. This is as trite a way to end a melody as exists, but the context changed that totally. My mother was a music teacher, and she instilled in me an acute sensitivity to harmonic resonances. When that acquisition and my Christian nurturance converged on the Good Friday story under psilocybin, the gestalt transformed a routine musical progression into the most powerful cosmic homecoming I have ever experienced.

Having indicated how I experienced the service I can turn now to the incident that is the main point of this interview.

As the psilocybin began to take its effect, I became aware of a mounting disorder in the chapel. After all, half of our number were in a condition where social decorum meant nothing, and the other half were more interested in the spectacle that was unfolding before them than in the service proper. In any case, from out of this bizarre mix, one of our number emerged. He arose from his pew, walked up the aisle, and with uncertain steps mounted the chapel's modest pulpit. Thumbing through its Bible for a few moments, he proceeded to mumble a brief and incoherent homily, blessed the congregation with the sign of the cross, and started back down the aisle. But instead of returning to his pew, he marched to the rear entrance of the chapel and through its door.

Now, before the experiment began, we had been arranged in groups of four subjects plus two guides. We knew that two subjects and one guide in each group would receive psilocybin, and the guides were instructed to look after the others as needed. "John" (I withhold his actual name) was not my charge, but as no one got up to follow him, I did so.

This introduces an interesting parenthetical point. More than once I have been struck by the widely corroborated fact that however deep one may be into the chemical experience, short of the dissociation that John was experiencing, one can snap back to normal if need arises to so do. So it was in this case. When John's guide didn't respond to his leaving the chapel, I sprang to my feet and followed him out.

He had made a right turn and was striding down the hall, but that didn't worry me because we had been told that the entire basement had been sealed off for the experiment. But when he reached the door at the end of the corridor and jammed down its latch bar, it swung open. Something had misfired in the instructions to the janitor, and my charge, totally transported by his altered state, was loose on Commonwealth Avenue. I ran after him, but my remonstrances to return to the chapel fell on deaf ears, and he shook off my grip as if it were cobwebs.

What to do? I was afraid to leave him lest I lose track of him, but alone I was powerless to dissuade him from what appeared to be an appointed mission.

Providentially, help arrived from an unexpected quarter. Eva Pahnke, Wally's wife, was having a picnic on the grass with their child, and I shouted to her to keep track of John while I rushed back to the chapel for help. The strategy worked. When I returned on the double with Wally and another helper, John was still visible a block and a half ahead. Before we reached him we saw him enter what turned out to be 745 Commonwealth Avenue, the building that houses Boston University's School of Theology and parts of its College of Liberal Arts. We caught up with him on the stairs to the third floor, but Wally's remonstrances cut no more ice than mine had. Together, however, the three of us were able to block his further ascent.

Things were at a standstill when a postman rounded the corner of the steps from below. He was carrying a brown envelope copiously plastered with special-delivery stickers, and as he was passing us John's arm shot out and snatched it from him. I was too occupied to notice the expression on the postman's face, for two of us had all we could do pinning John's arms while finger by finger, Wally pried the crumpled envelope from John's viselike grip and returned it to its stunned carrier. I have often wondered how that postman explained the mangled condition of his packet to its recipient, and how he described the incident to his wife at dinner that evening.

The rest is simply told. Realizing that he was overpowered – barely, for under the influence his strength was like Samson's – John, tightly flanked, submitted to being walked back to the chapel where Wally injected thorazine, an antidote. That returned him to his right mind, but with no recollection of what had happened. It took twenty-four hours for all the pieces of the episode to come back to him and fall into place, whereupon this was his story.

God, it emerged, had chosen him to announce to the world the dawning of the Messianic Age, a millennium of universal peace. (As often happens in such cases, the actual wording of the message made little sense to normal ears.) In his homily in the chapel, John broke the good news to our congregation, but he needed to get it to the world at large, which was what caused him to leave the chapel. When, walking down Commonwealth Avenue, he saw the plaque announcing "Dean of the College of Liberal Arts" by the entrance to 745 Commonwealth Avenue, it occurred to him that deans have influence, so if he could get to him, the dean would call a press conference that would complete John's mission. The postman's packet, he assumed, was for the dean, so if he attached himself to it, it would carry him to the dean himself.

John's long-term feelings about the experiment were heavily negative. He was the only one of its subjects who refused to participate
in Rick Doblin's twenty-fifth-year retrospective study of the long-
term effects of the experiment on its subjects, and he threatened to
sue if his name was included.

ROBERTS

Was there something in Howard Thurman's sermon that
prompted him to his messianic mission?

SMITH

Not to my notice. It was a typical Good Friday service with med-
itations on each of the seven last words of Christ. Howard Thurman was a remarkable man, both spiritually and in his ability to in-
spire people, but I don't remember the content of his words, only
their moving impact. Did you ever meet him?

ROBERTS

No. I wish I had.

SMITH

Just relating this story I feel my spine tingling.

ROBERTS

Are there other memories of the afternoon that come to mind?

SMITH

I come back to the hubbub that erupted at times in our chapel.
I was too deep into my own experience to be distracted by it, but I
was peripherally aware of it and realized in retrospect that an observer would have found us a pretty unruly bunch. Half of us were
enraptured, while the other half (as I learned from several of them
the next day) felt left out and were not above acting out their re-
sentment in derisive laughter and incredulous hoots over the way
the rest of us were behaving.

I also recall a short exchange with one of our number in the foy-
er to the chapel just before the service began. I was already feeling
my psilocybin, and sensing – wrongly, it turned out – that he was
as well, I said to him from the depths of my being, "It's true, isn't
it?" By "it," I meant the religious outlook, God and all that follows

from God's reality. He didn't respond and told me when we next met that he had gotten only the placebo and hadn't a clue as to what I was talking about. So I was dead wrong in inferring from our eye contact that our minds were in sync.

ROBERTS

Anything else?

SMITH

Only the gratitude I feel toward Wally for having mounted the experiment – as you know, it's a poignant gratitude for he died nine years later in a tragic scuba diving accident. I have explained how it enlarged my understanding of God by affording me the only powerful experience I have had of his personal nature. I had known and firmly believed that God is love and that none of love's nuances could be absent from his infinite nature; but that God loves *me*, and I *him*, in the concrete way that human beings love individuals, each most wanting from the other what the other most wants to give and with everything that might distract from that holy relationship excluded from view – *that* relation with God I had never before had. It's the theistic mode that doesn't come naturally to me, but I have to say for it that its car-ryover topped those of my other entheogenic epiphanies. From somewhere between six weeks and three months (I should judge) I really *was* a better person – even at this remove, I remain confident of that. I slowed down a bit and was somewhat more considerate. I was able to some extent to prolong the realization that life really is a miracle, every moment of it, and that the only appropriate way to respond to the gift that we have been given is to be mindful of that gift at every moment and to be caring toward everyone we meet. To carry those sentiments with one onto the campus of the Massachusetts Institute of Technology requires empowerment.

ROBERTS

Thank you, Huston.

SMITH

You are welcome.

The Case of Cardinal John Henry Newman

Twenty years had elapsed since I had last written about the entheogens, and I might have kept my peace had not the editors of the journal ReVISION dedicated one of its 1988 issues to the topic and requested an entry from me. My initial impulse was to decline, thinking that I had said all I had to say on the subject, but then I remembered that I had come upon a significant item in the interval that I had not reported. It relates to a towering nineteenth-century intellect, Cardinal John Henry Newman, and I used my entry for ReVISION to tell the story.

For their relevance to the Newman story, I have (in this printing of it) added Dostoevsky's conclusions about his epilepsy. I urge the reader not miss those conclusions, as he might be likely to do because they appear in a footnote (I have placed them in that category only to keep them from interrupting the flow of the central, Newman narrative). Far from being incidental, Dostoevsky's perplexity and "paradoxical conclusion" (which he camouflages as fiction in The Idiot) are so close to the ones that have kept me circling the entheogens for forty years that I could easily have paraphrased them to provide a completely satisfying rationale for my publishing this book.

I thought that I had published everything I have to say about the entheogens, but ReVISION's invitation to contribute to this issue of the journal reminds me that there is one item that has come my way which I have not seen reported. I begin with the circumstances that brought it to light, and I shall dwell on them somewhat, for the improbabilities involved are enough to remind one once again of life's strangeness. If this had not occurred, and that – and that, and that, and that, each in its seemingly appointed time and place – a pertinent fact about

John Henry Newman's conversion might never have come to light.

The story centers in the three-week Salzburg Seminar of 1972. Endowed by an Austrian immigrant to the United States who used the fortune he made to throw a bridge from his native homeland to the country that had treated him well, these seminars, which take place annually, are designed to inform influential Europeans about current aspects of American life, and the turbulent sixties drew me into their orbit. Taken together, the convulsive events of that decade – civil rights demonstrations (Martin Luther King), protests against the war in Vietnam (Daniel Ellsberg), musical breakthroughs (Bob Dylan and the Beatles), and Woodstock with its flower children and summer of love – led the public to reify the decade, making it a freestanding thing in itself. And because psychedelics (Timothy Leary and Haight-Ashbury) were a flamboyant part of that decade and I had paid more attention to them than had most academics, I was invited to be one of the four leaders of the 1972 seminar. Martin Marty, Robert McAfee Brown, and Michael Novak dealt with the civil rights revolution and Vietnam, while I did what I could to interpret the rise of the counterculture in America with its psychedelics included. One of the participants in the seminar, Hillary Jenkins, had just completed a book on John Henry Newman, *Newman's Mediterranean Voyage,* and when his knowledge of Newman's life intersected with what I was telling the seminar about the entheogens, some disparate pieces coalesced in a hypothesis that startled us all.

I begin with Jenkins's part of the story. In researching Newman's life, Jenkins learned that in his early twenties he had been severely depressed. He had no idea what to do with his life and was plagued by a crippling anxiety in which he oscillated between fear of failure on the one hand and an ambitious but daunting desire to advance himself on the other. In the hope of relieving his depression, his parents sent him on a Mediterranean vacation, and their plan succeeded in a way no one could have anticipated. In the course of his vacation he had a religious experience that was so powerful that not only did it pull him out of his depression, it caused him quickly to become a public figure and made him in time an intellectual giant of his century. His *Idea of the University* is still regarded as one of the best books on education ever written. "Lead, Kindly Light" is one of Christendom's best-loved hymns. And Newman Centers – his tangible memorial – grace every major college and university campus in America.

The interests of this book enter when we learn that the experience that literally turned Newman into a "new man" occurred in the course of a near-fatal bout with a disease now judged to have been typhoid fever, and that Newman himself was aware in retrospect that (in his own words) "at the time that I had a most consoling and overpowering thought of God's electing love and seemed to feel I was His, all my feelings, painful and pleasant, were, I believe, heightened somewhat by delirium."

Here my own studies entered the picture, specifically something I picked up at a conference on psychoactive substances that the R. M. Bucke Society convened in Canada in the late 1960s. In the paper that Raymond Prince – a medical anthropologist in the Section of Transcultural Psychiatric Studies at McGill University – presented at that conference, he argued that infectious diseases, and other afflictions such as starvation and exhaustion on long hunting expeditions, probably figured more prominently than hallucinogenic plants in opening early man to the supernatural. These afflictions, too, affect brain chemistry in visionary directions and probably beset people quite regularly.* The bacteria

---

* Prince does not mention the brain states that immediately precede epileptic fits, but it seems reasonable to include them in his list. Dostoevsky's generalized description of the experience that accompanies those states – which he knew at first hand and which he puts in the mouth of Myshkin in *The Idiot* – has become classic: "[Myshkin] remembered among other things that he always had one minute just before the epileptic fit (if it came on while he was awake), when suddenly in the midst of sadness, spiritual darkness and oppression, there came at moments a flash of light in his brain, and with extraordinary impetus all his vital forces suddenly began working at their highest tension. The sense of life, the consciousness of self, were multiplied ten times at these moments which passed like a flash of lightning. His mind and his heart were flooded with extraordinary light; all his uneasiness, all his doubts, all his anxieties were relieved at once; they were all merged in a lofty calm, full of serene, harmonious joy and hope. But these moments, these flashes,

and other micro-organisms that cause infectious diseases are themselves plants and fungi, or closely akin to them. Moreover, it is they (not the fever their attacks provoke) that account for the visions that occur, for (a) deliriums may precede temperature rise and follow its return to normal, (b) fevers experimentally produced without infectious organisms do not alter consciousness, and (c) some febrile illnesses occasion deliriums, whereas

were only the prelude of that final second (it was never more than a second) with which the fit began. That second was, of course, unendurable. Thinking of that moment later, when he was all right again, he often said to himself that all these gleams and flashes of the highest sensation of life and self-consciousness, and therefore also of the highest form of existence, were nothing but disease, the interruption of the normal conditions; and if so, it was not at all the highest form of being, but on the contrary must be reckoned the lowest. And yet he came at last to an extremely paradoxical conclusion. 'What if it is a disease?' he decided at last. 'What does it matter that it is an abnormal intensity, if the result, if the minute of sensation, remembered and analyzed afterwards in health, turns out to be the acme of harmony and beauty, and gives a feeling, unknown and undivined till then, of completeness, of proportion, of reconciliation and of ecstatic devotional merging in the highest synthesis of life?' These vague expressions seemed to him very comprehensible, though too weak. That it really was 'beauty and worship,' that it really was the 'highest synthesis of life' he could not doubt, and could not admit the possibility of doubt. It was not as though he saw abnormal and unreal visions of some sort at that moment, as from hashish, opium, or wine, destroying the reason and distorting the soul. He was quite capable of judging of that when the attack was over. These moments were only an extraordinary quickening of self-consciousness – if the condition was to be expressed in one word – and at the same time of the direct sensation of existence in the most intense degree. Since at that second, that is at the very last conscious moment before the fit, he had time to say to himself clearly and consciously, 'Yes, for this moment one might give one's whole life!' then without doubt that moment was really worth the whole of life. He did not insist on the dialectical part of his argument, however. Stupefaction, spiritual darkness, idiocy stood before him conspicuously as the consequence of these 'higher moments'; seriously, of course, he could not have disputed it. There was undoubtedly a mistake in his conclusion – that is in his estimate of that minute, but the reality of the sensation somewhat perplexed him. What was he to make of that reality? For the very thing had happened; he actually had said to himself at that second, that, for the infinite happiness he had felt in it, that second really might be worth the whole of life. 'At that moment,' as he told Rogozhin one day in Moscow at the time when they used to meet there, 'at that moment I seem somehow to understand the extraordinary saying that *there shall be no more time*. Probably,' he added smiling, 'this is the very second which was not long enough for the water to be spilt out of Mahomet's pitcher, though the epileptic prophet had time to gaze at all the habitations of Allah.'"

others do not – smallpox, typhoid, and pneumonia fall into the first category; diphtheria, tetanus, and cholera into the second.

From this important paragraph, two relevant points emerge. The first – that austerities, including starvation and exhaustion, can cause somatic changes which at minimum accompany dramatic theophanies – has been known for some time and has been well covered; one thinks of Moses neither eating nor drinking for forty days on Mount Horeb before he saw the mountain in flames, and Christ's forty days in the wilderness where he too fasted for forty days and forty nights before Satan appeared visibly to him with his three temptations. What is new here is the prospect that an infectious disease may have opened John Henry Newman to his life-transforming visitation.

My brief entry for *ReVISION* concluded with that paragraph, but in the context of this book I will append this coda.

Some will find disturbing the conclusion that the facts here point toward; namely, that the religious experience that produced a giant of the Roman Catholic Church seems to have occurred while Newman was undergoing an entheogenic disease. To some extent I am in their company, and if it turns out that the facts fuel "the hermeneutics of suspicion" more than they serve the cause of truth, I shall regret not having kept them to myself. But in a dramatically incisive way, those facts highlight the basic object of this book, which is to ask if it is possible to honor the noetic deliverances of entheogenic theophanies without contradicting what we know about brain chemistry.

Newman himself faced that question at its incipient stage, and I respect the way he answered it. After acknowledging (as above reported) that his delirium may have heightened his feelings when he sensed that God had him under his care and had marked him for leadership, he went on to add, "but they still are from God in the way of Providence."

Entheogenic Religions:
The Eleusinian Mysteries and
the Native American Church

In the effort to see what the entheogens have to teach us about what we human beings are (human nature), about the inclusive context in which we live our lives (the world), and about the connection between the two (religion), the essays in this book approach those interlocking issues from various angles. This chapter touches on two instances where they produced full-fledged religions. Chapter 4 anticipated this topic, for Soma figured prominently in Hinduism's formation, but the concern in that chapter was restricted to the plant's botanical identity.

Beginning with the Eleusinian Mysteries, the first part of this chapter reprints the Preface to the revised edition of Wasson, Ruck, and Hofmann's groundbreaking book, The Road to Eleusis (Los Angeles: Hermes Press, 1998). I was especially pleased to have been asked to write that Preface, for I am a Platonist at heart, and it seems likely that Plato's basic outlook derived from his Eleusinian initiation.

My involvement with the Native American Church is a longer story. A former student of mine works for the Native American Rights Fund, and when in 1990 the United States Supreme Court ruled that the First Amendment does not guarantee a right to use peyote, he asked me if I wanted to become involved. I said that I did, and spent the next two years helping a remarkable Native American leader, Reuben Snake, compile a book titled One Nation Under God: The Triumph of the Native American Church (Santa Fe: Clear Light Publishers, 1996). It originated with a political aim – to help win the right in all fifty states for the sacramental use of Peyote – but things moved faster than we had expected, and before the book went to press the Church had established its right through Congress. This caused us to turn the book into a celebration of the Native Americans' victory over the highest court of the land, and an account (for the historical record) of the impressive but little-publicized movement the Native Americans mounted to realize their aim.

My chief contribution to that book was to interview members of the Native American Church in a number of its tribal branches to discover what the Church meant to them. The second half of this chapter presents samples of their testimonials, included here to show how the faith that entheogens generate can reach proportions that virtually require its institutionalization, even if only in the decentralized, congregational fashion of the Native American Church.

First, my Preface to the Eleusis book.

Two allegories frame Western civilization like majestic bookends – Plato's Allegory of the Cave at its start, and for now, Nietzsche's madman charging through the streets announcing that God is dead. We should not be sanguine about the direction in which those two landmarks point, for the notion of what it means to be human is far lower in the second allegory than in the first. "We do not think well of ourselves," Saul Bellow told his audience in accepting his Nobel Laureate prize, and he was right. Plato tells us that when his vision of reality swept him up and he sensed its life-giving implications, "First a shudder runs through me, and then the old awe creeps over me." Today we have the eminent physicist Steven Weinberg's report, "The more intelligible we find the universe, the more meaningless it seems."

Athens, of course, is only one of the sources of western civilization, its companion being Jerusalem whose assessment of things is as impressive as Athens'. We need only think of Moses trembling with awe on seeing Mount Sinai in flames; of Isaiah beholding the Lord high and lifted up, filling the whole earth with his glory; and of Jesus to whom the heavens opened at his baptism. To contrast this again with modernity, only recently has it come to light (through Frau Overbeck's report in *Conversations with Nietzsche*) that Nietzsche was himself deeply troubled by the loss that his madman reported. He was not sure that humanity could survive godlessness.

The bearing of all this on the book in hand is quite direct. Some theophanies seem to occur spontaneously, while others are facilitated by ways that seekers have discovered – one thinks of the place of fasting in the vision quest, the nightlong dancing of the Kalahari bushmen, prolonged intonings of sacred mantras, and the way peyote figures in the all-night vigils of the Native American Church. We do not know if (on the human side) it was anything more than absolute faith that joined earth to heaven on Mount Sinai and when three of Jesus' disciples saw him transfigured on Mount Hermon, his face shining like the sun and his clothes dazzling white. The Greeks, though, created a holy institution, the Eleusinian Mysteries, which seems regularly to have opened a space in the human psyche for God to enter.

The content of those Mysteries is, together with the identity of India's sacred Soma plant, one of the two best-kept secrets in history, and this book is the most successful attempt I know to unlock it. Triangulating the resources of an eminent classics scholar, Carl A. P. Ruck; the most creative mycologist of our time, R. Gordon Wasson; and the discoverer of LSD, Albert Hofmann, it is a historical tour de force while being more than that. For by direct implication it raises contemporary questions which our cultural establishment has thus far deemed too hot to handle.

The first of these is the already-cited question Nietzsche raised: Can humanity survive godlessness, which is to say, the lack of ennobling vision – a convincing, inspiring view of the nature of things and life's place in it?

Second, have modern secularism, scientism, materialism, and consumerism conspired to form a carapace that Transcendence now has difficulty piercing? If the answer to that second question is affirmative, a third one follows hard on its heels.

Is there need, perhaps an urgent need, to devise something like the Eleusinian Mysteries to get us out of Plato's cave and into the light of day?

Finally, can a way be found to legitimize, as the Greeks did, the constructive, life-giving use of entheogenic heaven-and-hell drugs without aggravating our serious drug problem?

The Road to Eleusis does not answer (or even directly address) these important, possibly fateful, questions. What it does do is to raise them by clear implication, elegantly and responsibly.

I turn now to the testimonials of members of the Native American Church, preceding them with the two opening paragraphs of the Preface that I wrote for the book from which the testimonials are drawn.

In a place apart, closer to nature than to the human scene, a tepee throws its outline against the night sky, a sacred silhouette. Inside, thirty or so Indians, men and women, sit on blankets and mats around a fire. Several children are sleeping in their parents' laps or on the ground by their sides. A seven-stone water drum pounds loudly and rapidly – the fetal heartbeat raised to cosmic proportions. Songs are sung with piercing intensity, interspersed with prayers and confessions. Tears flow, and a sacrament is ingested. It is a congregation of the Native American Church in one of its appointed meetings.

The Native American Church is the spiritual bulwark of an estimated quarter-million of the original inhabitants of this continent. Its roots extend into the twilight zone of prehistory, before the rise of Christianity or any of the historical religions.

[The testimonials that now unfold begin with one by Reuben Snake, who co-edited the book from which they are drawn.]

I am a Hochunk or Winnebago, and the Native American Church has been the center of my adult life. Everything we do in our Church is to honor the Creator and find our place in his creation. We try to respect and honor our families and friends; we try to have compassion for our fellow men, for that's what our Creator tells us to do. This attitude comes to us through a sacred herb, one that is sacred because it is, in fact, divine. We call it Peyote, but more often, because of what it does for us, we call it our Medicine. It is the most powerful of all the plants, because God endowed it with his love and compassion. He put those qualities into this lowly herb so that when we eat it we can feel that the love that God is – I emphasize the love that God *is*, not that God *has* – is physically inside us. From there it overflows in compassion for human beings and all other kinds of creatures. It enables us to treat one another tenderly, and with joy, love, and respect.

[I continue with the remaining testimonials I have selected, arranged according to the aspect of peyote that each addresses most directly.]

The Medicine

We can't explain our religion. To understand it you have to eat its Medicine.

—Anonymous

Our favorite term for Peyote is Medicine. To us it is a portion of the body of Christ, even as the communion bread is believed to be a portion of Christ's body for Christians.

In the Bible, Christ spoke of a comforter who was to come. Sent by God, this comforter came to the Indians in the form of this holy Medicine. We know whereof we speak. We have tasted of God and our eyes have been opened.

It is utter folly for scientists to attempt to analyze this Medicine. Can science analyze God's body? It is a part of God's body, and God's Holy Spirit envelops it. It cures us of our temporal ills, as well as ills of a spiritual nature. It takes away the desire for strong drink. I myself have been cured of a loathsome disease too horrible to mention. So have hundreds of others. Hundreds of confirmed drunkards have been rescued from their downward ways.

—Albert Hensley, Winnebago

I'll be ninety-four on my next birthday, so if there's an example of someone who's been using Peyote all his life, I guess I am he. I feel that I would die for this Medicine, it has meant so much to my life. My people use it and find spiritual guidance. When I sit in the tepee and partake of the Medicine, I concentrate and think. I think of how I want to be blessed and who I want to pray for. The outside world disappears. I feel humble, and the good thoughts that come to me help me.

—Truman Dailey, Otoe-Missouri

I have never seen colors or experienced delusions of any sort while taking Peyote. What it feels like is that I am sitting right by God the Creator. I communicate with him. Of course he isn't there physically, but spiritually I sense that he is near me. And whatever I pray for, I feel that he hears me. Other than that special sense of closeness, the experience isn't remarkable.

Part of the experience of being close to God is that the Medicine gets bad stuff out of you. If you have evil thoughts or are in a poor frame of mind generally, you are going to see all that clearly. In this way, if you're not living your life well, Peyote purifies you. It helps clean your spirit. I have heard many testimonials of gratitude to the Creator and prayers for forgiveness.

—Patricia Mousetail Russell,
Southern Cheyenne

The Medicine is the main thing of all. It's our life. Nothing else can accomplish much without the herb the Creator gave us.

—A Washoe

Peyote is power. A tremendous power pervades the tepee during a meeting. It will take all your lifetime to know only a small part of the power that is there.

—Similar statements by a Navajo and
Crow, here interwoven

In the first creation God himself used to talk to people and tell them what to do. Long after, Christ came among the white people and told them what to do. Then God gave us Indians Peyote. That's how we found God.

—A Kiowa

Peyote goes all over my body – I feel it, its workings. My mind is clear. Before I didn't think much about what's right, but with Peyote I know it's God working, the God who gave it to us. I feel good because God is going to take care of me. I have nothing to worry about, nothing to be afraid of because the Almighty is at work.

—Dewey Neconish, Menomini

Reverence, Humility, Awe, and Love

There are certain times in a meeting when you can feel a presence. It's a holy feeling, the presence of the spirit of God that's in the midst of these people. It makes you want to pray deep in your heart.

—A Menomini man in his forties

Last week we admitted a newspaperwoman who wanted to find out about the Native American Church. When she came out of the tepee in the morning she told us how humble she felt. That's true of us too. Our Holy Sacrament, Peyote, teaches us humility.

—Paris Williams, Ponca

That night I realized that in all the years that I had lived on earth I had never known anything holy. Now, for the first time, I knew something holy.

—John Rave, Winnebago, after his
first Peyote meeting

I'm glad I joined the Native American Church and used the Medicine, since it makes me think about the Almighty and how far away I have gotten from him.

—Beatrice Weasel Bear

Sometimes I am sitting here at home all alone, but I am not alone. I have my drum, water, and a gourd. I sing the songs of my church and my worries are gone. I feel good again, and refreshed. Peyote is not like a narcotic. When you eat it, your mind turns to the Great Spirit.

—Bernard Ice, a blind Oglala Lakota

Peyote to me is my Bible. I know what I should be doing and shouldn't be doing. When I take that Peyote, I feel humble and respectful all the time.

—Larry Etsitty, Navajo

This Medicine's got hope in it. It's got faith in it. It's got love in it. And it's got charity in it. So fill up all the fireplaces. Fill them up with those four words.

—Willie Riggs, Sr., Navajo Roadman

Moral Impact

This Peyote has done me a world of good. It put me on the right road. It has caused me to put aside all intoxicating liquor. I now have no desire for whiskey, beer, or any strong drink. I have no desire for tobacco. If I keep on using this Peyote, I'm going to be an upright man toward God.

—A Menomini

When I started eating that Medicine it told me something. I found out I was a sinner. Then I commenced to think why I was like that. I ate some more, and I found out that Peyote teaches me what is right. From then on I've tried to behave myself.

—A Menomini

Chief Peyote tells us that our meetings are to make Indians good, to make them friends, and to make them stop fighting. When we eat Peyote we feel towards others a warm glow in our hearts as if they were our brothers.

—Ralph Kochampanaskin

This is all that I know. When I started eating this Medicine I began to see everything. I no longer quarreled with anyone. I no longer was angry with anyone. That's it. When I started to eat this Medicine I began to think of the Great Spirit always, every day.

—A Menomini woman in her seventies

Petition, Prayer, Thanksgiving, and Guidance

Well Great Spirit, the time has now come. I am going to pray to you where I am standing. Please let everything be abundant, so that we may exist well on this earth where we live. We thank you, Great Spirit above, for allowing us to live up to the present. We pray you to give strength to every one of us. Hold the hands of each one of my children. Give them strength. Give them that which is good in the future, and make them stand erect here on earth where we live.

—An anonymous Menomini

Great Spirit who is all, I am going to give you thanks now. And now I am telling you in advance that we have all come here to this house, which you gave us, to pray to be purified. Now we are going to enter to pray to you all night. These, my brothers and sisters, will pray to you. Please keep carefully in mind whatever they will ask of you. Also, my relatives have come to visit us. They are going to pray to you for whatever is in their thoughts. So in advance we are telling you, here, that we are going to enter this house which you have given us to pray to you.

—Thomas Wayka, Menomini

Healing

I am ninety-six years old now, and when people ask me how long I have been taking this Medicine I say since before I was born. I say that because my mother took some Peyote the night before she delivered me. First she offered a prayer, and then she swallowed the Medicine. I was born about noon the following day, and as soon as she could get up and around, the first thing she did was make some Medicine tea and give me some of it. To understand all this you need to know that I wasn't her first child. There had been two boys before me, but neither of them survived. My mother wanted to be sure that I would make it, and that's why she took the Medicine at the time of my delivery and gave me some as soon as she was able.

To help you understand her great faith in our Medicine I have to go back four or five years. About three years before she gave birth to me she got so she couldn't walk, and to explain what happened then I need to go back still farther and tell you about her upbringing.

Her mother – my grandmother – was an orphan who was brought up in a Christian way and raised my mother that way. But when she was of marriageable age she went to visit the nearby Otoe tribe. One of the boys there liked her and they got married. The family she married into was one hundred percent Indian, but her upbringing had been Christian. Then a strange malady beset her. The doctors never did understand what it was, but she became crippled. She couldn't walk. With her Christian upbringing she prayed as hard as she could to Jesus, but she kept getting worse.

Then something happened that turned out to be important. Her family was on its way to a tribal meeting of some sort and the house where they stopped to spend the night had a tepee behind it – there was going to be a Peyote meeting that night. That was the first Peyote meeting my mother had ever attended. Around midnight a bucket of water was passed around and she drank some. That water hadn't touched the ground because it had been collected in pans that people had put out to catch rain. After they drank the water they stared to sing, and then they offered my mother the Medicine. They told her that if she took the Medicine and prayed with all the faith she could manage, it might help her. She consumed it, prayed, and when the meeting was over she began to get well. Within a month she was walking.

I don't know, of course, but it seems like her faith was equally strong when she was a Christian, but when she got on the Indian side of religion and took the Medicine, it seems like that's what made the difference and enabled her to walk again.

—Truman Dailey

Two years ago I fell ill. It was scary because I seemed to have a blood disorder. The doctors were talking about sending me to Minnesota to have me treated for leukemia.

Four days before my birthday my parents put on a prayer service for me. They rolled the sacred tobacco, gave me Medicine, fanned me with the waterbird fan, and prayed for me. Four days later I went to the hospital. My blood count was normal and I gained back the weight I had lost.

I think too of the miracle that happened to my Grandpa

Philip from whom I get my middle name, Afraid-of-Bear. Once when he was home on leave from the service there was a prayer ceremony for a young man who was desperately ill. Grandpa was the Fireman at this meeting and Peyote was placed in the center of the room so everybody could eat as much as they wanted. In ceremonies that are specifically for healing, people ingest as much as they can, and more, to increase the Medicine's power.

As the evening wore on, it seemed clear that the young man was dying. So when midnight arrived and it was time for Grandpa to pray officially as Fireman, he asked the creator to take his goodness, his wholesomeness and his strength, and give them to the younger, dying man. He said he would be willing to lay down his remaining years for the man, who had not experienced as much of life as he had.

The young man survived his crisis and did pull through. But Grandpa! The next day, while chasing horses, he keeled over with a heart attack. That was sad, but it happened the way he wanted it to. Peyote listened to him, and granted what he asked.

—Loretta Afraid-of-Bear Cook, Lakota

New Life and Behavior Change

I started using Peyote when I came back from the army in 1962. I stopped using liquor because it is not right to use it with the Medicine. I told all these people when they came to my meeting, you guys better straighten up. This liquor doesn't go with Medicine. White people say liquor and gas don't go together and it's the same with Medicine. Liquor and Medicine don't go together.

—Irvine Tachonie, Navajo

It's been twenty-three years that I've lived a life of sobriety. I don't smoke cigarettes like I used to. I don't drink alcohol or use any kind of drugs because of the life that I now live in the Native American Church. That's what it's done for me, for my family and my relatives on both sides: my Winnebago in-laws, my Sioux relatives, my Menomini relatives, my Creek and Seminole and Ottawa and Iowa, my people back home in Oklahoma.

—Johnny White Cloud, Otoe-
Missouri/Creek/Seminole

I'm into my sixth year of recovery from alcoholism. I'm off the bottle now, but the temptation is still there. When I go to Peyote I pray God to forgive my old alcoholism and to keep me sober.

Over the years Peyote has taught me many things, though actually it is God who taught them to me through Peyote.

—Andy Kozad, Kiowa

When I first used Peyote I became deathly sick. It seemed like I vomited several bottles of whiskey, several plugs of tobacco, and two bulldogs. This accumulation of filth represented all the sins I had ever committed. With its expulsion I became pure and clean in the sight of God, and I knew that by the continued use of Peyote I would remain in that condition. I was transformed – a new man.

—A Winnebago

My heart was filled with murderous thoughts when I first took Peyote. I wanted to kill my brother and sister. All my thoughts were fixed on the warpath. Some evil spirit possessed me. I even desired to kill myself.

Then I ate this Medicine and everything changed. I became deeply attached to the brother and sister whom I had wanted to kill. This the Medicine accomplished for me.

—John Rave

Women and the Feminine

A long time ago one of my aunts, Ethel Blackbird, told me that Peyote can be used for many kinds of healings and that we should take it when we have our babies.

When it came time for me to do the woman's ritual of having my first child, my mother came from Washington State where she had been living. My labor pains started around four in the morning and she immediately got up and gave me some Medicine. This pulled my resources back inside of me and kept me calm. Being calm enabled me to experience the birthing process clearly and calmly, consciously sensing and feeling what was going on.

—Loretta Afraid-of-Bear Cook

Bereavement and Death

Many people have gone on the path of this life and beyond. Our altar, which is in the shape of a mound, is Mother Earth where you come from and where you return. It is the same as the biblical passage, "from dust to dust." As you eat Peyote, the altar becomes a grave into which many a man has gone.

—Lawrence Hunter, Minneconjou Lakota

My grandmother wanted her Last Sacraments. They were going to call a minister, but she said she wanted them in the Peyote way. William Black Bear gave her four Peyote balls, and my father sang four songs. They said the Lord's Prayer, and she said Amen and breathed her last breath.

—Eva Gap, Oglala Lakota

Something Like a Summing-Up

The tentativeness expressed in the title of this concluding chapter is emphatic, for in rereading the essays in this book I realize that I am no closer today to answering the central problem they circle – given what we now know about brain chemistry, can entheogenic visions be validated as true? – than I was after my first encounter with them almost forty years ago. All I can do is stuff into the duffel bag a few remaining items I think should be included and then pull its drawstrings and knot them.

Three encounters with the entheogens – none of them mine – have crossed my path that seem significant enough to relate. Two of them were positive, the other negative, and I begin with the hell side of these heaven-and-hell substances.

In 1962 I delivered the first of what has become an annual Charles Strong Lecture on World Religions to the universities of Australia. The appointment called for spending three or four days at each university, and (as the Harvard psilocybin research was still in place and had attracted global attention) several of my hosts raised the subject with me. Some months after my return to Cambridge, an Australian who had been party to one of these conversations turned up on my doorstep. He was carrying LSD that was burning a hole in his pocket, but he was reserving it for Niagara Falls, which he had targeted as the perfect place for his initiation. His plan – to ingest capsules of unknown dosage alone in a potentially dangerous physical setting – struck terror in my heart, but there was no stopping him. His mind was made up. He was on his way to what, from hearsay, he was certain was going to be the peak experience of his life.

Several days passed and then my phone rang. It was a collect call – would I accept charges? The operator wasn't altogether clear as to who was calling, but it was someone in Buffalo, and, suspecting immediately his identity, I accepted the call. There was a long silence, and then an agitated voice kicked in. I couldn't make heads or tails of what it was saying. Garbled sentences would be left hanging in midair and replaced by other false starts until the whole dissolved into sobs and wails. There was a desperate, prolonged cry of "Hooooooooston" which trailed off into nothingness and the line went dead.

It wasn't until several days later when two police officers appeared at my door that the story emerged. The police had gotten involved when, on the rim of Niagara Falls, "John" (I forget his actual name) exposed himself publicly. Converging on him and finding him incoherent, the officers handcuffed him, whereupon he snapped the chain – a first in the cops' experience. John was behind bars in Buffalo awaiting a hearing. Somewhere down the line I heard that he had gotten into a serious legal scrape for having imported drugs which by then were illegal. That was the last I heard of the matter.

The other two stories have happier endings.

In Kathmandu in 1976, my wife and I heard that there was an American in a nearby Buddhist nunnery, and, being curious, we looked her up. Her story was this.

Born of Russian aristocracy, she immigrated with her parents to the United States where (after winning a beauty contest in Cannes) she married a Hollywood mogul. At the time when the psychedelics broke over America she found her life completely empty. She felt trapped by her marriage and was depressed to the point of seriously thinking of ending her life. LSD presented itself as a straw she might latch on to, and she ended up having ten sessions in all. I remember her accounts of four of them.

From her initial session she emerged remembering nothing. Zero. Total amnesia. It was as if eleven hours had been excised from her life, with one proviso. She was certain – and remained certain as she told us the story – that it was the most important event of her life.

Somewhere down the line, a male friend persuaded her – pressured is more accurate – to take LSD under his guidance. He wanted her to undress, but she agreed only if he provided her with a sheet to wrap herself in. He was an experienced mountain climber, and the walls of his apartment were papered with giant blow-ups of Himalayan peaks. All she remembered from that session was that she turned into an iceberg and sat upright and motionless the entire night.

In her ninth session, her life passed before her as if on film, and with that rerun behind her, her tenth and final ingestion had no effect at all, despite the fact that the dosage was as strong as in her other sessions. The chemical could have been aspirin for all the difference it made, and she resolved to become a Buddhist nun, a move she had been contemplating for several months. The Dalai Lama asked her to wait for a year, which she spent wrapping up her racy jet-set life, whereupon he acceded to her request, and there she sat before us. Her head was shaven, and her thin robes and sandals made our padded armor against the Himalayan winter seem self-indulgent. Yet she was cheerful and gave every evidence of being at peace with herself.

My third account concerns Bill Wilson, the beloved founder of Alcoholics Anonymous. My acquaintance with him was limited to an afternoon in his hotel room in Kansas City and the lecture he gave to two thousand recovering alcoholics that evening, and I was no more than a bystander throughout, as I had driven Gerald Heard (who was in residence at Washington University at the time) to Kansas City so the two men could update their long-standing friendship. Even so, to have been in the presence of those two men for three consecutive hours was an unforgettable experience. Bill – no one ever called him either William or Wilson – mostly set the agenda. He had recently taken LSD and was under the compulsion (typical in the first weeks following the initiation) to talk about it. The reason I mention that afternoon is to report that he counted his entheogen experience as equal in the conviction it engendered to the conversion experience that led him to his founding Alcoholics Anonymous.

Moving from those three anecdotes into my final wrap-up, I will begin with something that puzzled me for a while but which I think I have pretty much resolved.

Why, when I count several of my entheogen experiences as being among the most important in my life, have I no desire to repeat them? On occasion I have gone so far as to rank them with family and world travel in what they have contributed to my understanding of things, yet – with the exception of peyote, which I took in the line of duty while working with the Native Americans as described in chapter 8 – it has been decades since I have taken an entheogen, and if someone were to offer me today a substance that (with no risk of producing a bummer) was guaranteed to carry me into the Clear Light of the Void and within fifteen minutes return me to normal with no adverse side effects, I would decline. Why?

Half of my answer lies in the healthy respect I have for the awe entheogens engender; in Gordon Wasson's blunt assertion in the frontispiece to this book, "awe is not fun." I understand Meister Eckhart completely when he says that "in joy *and terror* the Son is born" (emphasis mine). I speak only for myself, of course – that durable formula of set and setting again – but if I am honest I have to say (and age may figure in this) that I am afraid of the entheogens. I will take them again if need be, as I did with peyote, but the reasons would have to be compelling.

The second half of my answer is that I have other things to do. This may sound like a limp excuse for foregoing ecstasy, so I will invoke the Buddhist doctrine of the Six Realms of Existence to explain the force it has for me.

Metaphysically, that doctrine posits six kinds of beings and the realms they inhabit. (The doctrine can also be read psychologically as six states of mind that human beings keep recycling, but I will stick to its metaphysical reading.) The two populations that are relevant here are the demi-gods, who are always happy, and human beings, whose lot is harder but who are actually the best off of the six kinds of beings because they alone possess free will with its power to change things. (The four I haven't mentioned are instinct-ridden *animals*, fiercely envious *jealous gods*, insatiably greedy *hungry ghosts*, and *hell beings* who are ravaged by rage.) Blissed out on

Cloud Nine, the demi-gods are still subject to time, which means that sooner or later their holidays will end and they will find themselves back in the form of life from which they were granted temporary leaves. Only the human state opens onto *nirvana*, which is why one of the three things that Buddhists give thanks for each day is that they have been born into a human body.

I will not try to separate what is literal from what is figurative in this account; only its moral teaching interests me here for supporting my second reason for having no desire to revisit the entheogens. The Sufis speak of three ways to know fire: through hearsay, by seeing its flames, and by being burned by those flames. Had I not been burned by the totally Real, I would still be seeking it as knights sought the Grail and moths seek flame. As it is, it seems prudent to "work for the night is coming," as a familiar hymn advises. Alan Watts put the point more directly: "When you get the message, hang up the phone."

The downside of swearing off is, of course, the danger that the Reality that trumps everything while it is in full view will fade into a memory and become like Northern Lights – beautiful, but cold and far away. The problem besets all epiphanies; the psalmist's lament, "restore unto me the joy of my salvation," has already been quoted. During the three years of the Harvard experiments the entheogens were the most exciting thing in my intellectual life, but at this remove I have to work to get my head back into those years and revive the excitement. I suspect that there are thousands of people out there, possibly millions, who would have reached passionately for a book such as this had they come upon it soon after their first ingestion when they thought the world would never be the same again, but who at this remove find its subject interesting but no more than that.

The question comes down to which experiences we should try to keep in place as beacon lights to guide us and which we should let lapse. The intensity of the experience doesn't give us the answer, as this final personal anecdote of the book bears out.

When the first UFO craze swept America in the 1950s I was teaching at Washington University in St. Louis where the president of McDonnell Aircraft gave Chancellor Arthur Compton a grant to convene a conference on Science and Human Responsibility. Having himself headed the team of physicists at the University of Chicago that produced the first chain reaction of splitting atoms, Compton was able to attract world-class scientists of the order of Werner Heisenberg to the conference. I was enlisted to manage arrangements and produce a record of the event.

On the evening of the conference I was in my dean's office reviewing the checklist of things to be done. He was speaking, when suddenly, midway through a sentence, a look of horror swept over his face and he plunged for the window behind me. I whirled to follow him, at which point my account becomes embarrassingly corny because what we saw fit the UFO stereotype so exactly. Five illuminated saucers were sweeping in a semicircle across the leaden clouds of the late November evening sky – astonishingly close to our window, it seemed. They were moving so fast that they were out of sight almost before we saw them. We bolted into his secretary's office hoping to follow them from her window, but they were gone.

Without exchanging a look, we retraced our steps and resumed our chairs in his office where we sat in total silence without looking at each other for about five minutes. The reason I am telling this story is for what we experienced in those minutes. We felt shaken to our foundations. Finally, the dean bestirred himself, looked at me, and said, "Well, Huston: I'm a dean and you're in religion; they'll never believe us." We went our respective ways and never mentioned the matter again.

In its immediate force, that experience rivals that of the entheogens, but, unlike the latter it had no lasting impact, the obvious reason being that I don't believe in invading extraterrestrials. That disbelief leaves me suspecting that a naturalistic explanation for what we saw exists, even though I don't know what it might be – an aircraft's wings that were reflecting rays from the setting sun, perhaps? What the account points up is the way our basic beliefs adjudicate what we make of our experiences, a point the Victorian poet Ella Wheeler Wilcox captures beautifully in the following quatrain:

> One ship drives east and another drives west
> by the self-same gale that blows,

> 'Tis the set of the sail, and not the gale,
> that determines the way she goes.

I can think of no better way to close down the ruminations of this book than to describe as succinctly as I can the set of the sail that has vectored them.

I believe that when "set and setting" are rightly aligned, the basic message of the entheogens – that there is another Reality that puts this one in the shade – is true. There is no way that the prevailing view of the human self (which depicts it as an organism in an environment that has evolved purposelessly through naturalistic causes only) can accept that claim, which means that its Procrustean anthropology must go. That it will go, has been the critical (as distinct from constructive) burden of all my writing, for it rests on assumptions that are too arbitrary to escape scrutiny indefinitely.

Endings, though, are not the place for argument, so I will let Robert Frost deliver my parting shot. I do not see how anyone can deny that the traditional, theomorphic view of the human self which the entheogens endorse is nobler than the one that common sense and modern science (misread) have replaced it with. Whether the theomorphic view is true or not cannot be objectively determined, so all I can ask of the opposition is that it not equate noble views with wishful thinking. They can be as demanding of us as are their opposites, as Frost suggests in his poem "A Cabin in the Clearing."

In it he has two wraiths, Mist and Smoke, talking about an old woodcutter and his wife huddled together in a cottage in a small clearing it the forest.

> No one – not I – would give them up for lost
> Simply because they don't know where they are,

says Mist. To which Smoke replies,

> If the day ever comes when they know who
> They are, they may know better where they are,
> But who they are is too much to believe . . .

Secularization and the Sacred: The Contemporary Scene

This first appendix steps back from the entheogens proper to situate them in their modern social context. The essay was written thirty years ago as a chapter in The Religious Situation, *edited by Donald Cutler, and I have rewritten it considerably to adapt it to the concerns of this book. I have retained references that link it to the sixties for the concreteness they give to the piece.*

Religion has lost ground startlingly in the last decade, at least in the eyes of the general public in the United States. In 1957, 14 percent of a Gallup national sample was of the opinion that "religion is losing its influence." By 1962 the figure had risen to 31 percent, by 1965 to 45 percent, and by 1967 it stood at 57 percent. In ten short years the proportion of Americans who see religion as in retreat has quadrupled, jumping from one-seventh to over half the population. Yet squarely within this decade of seeming collapse, an astute sociologist, Robert Bellah, has observed that "the United States is experiencing at the moment something of a religious revival."

The cognitive dissonance occasioned by Gallup's statistics and Bellah's perception sets the problem for this paper. Is one of the two mistaken, or are sacred and secular related in ways that are sufficiently multivalent to allow both to be correct?

"Secular" characterizes regions of life that man understands and controls, not necessarily completely but (as the saying goes, and here it is exact) for all practical purposes.

Thus defined, secularization has increased steadily with the advance of civilization. Primitive man obviously managed or we wouldn't be here, but there was little in his life that he understood sufficiently to effect clean control over it. As a consequence his society was whole and sacred throughout. For tribal peoples, hunting and husbandry are sacred activities; Toda priests tend sacred buffaloes, and totemic rites bind Arunta hunters to their prey in ties that both expedite and legitimize their killing. Likewise with healing: Medicine men are both physicians and priests.

In civilizations the situation is otherwise. Whether we read "In God We Trust" on our currency as vestigial or as precise index of the extent to which the Almighty Dollar has become an object of worship, Western economies have become completely secular. We do not fully understand how economies work and so can only marginally control them, but we certainly don't charge their vagaries against God, any more than (short of desperation) we implicate him in health. Similarly with Medicine. Priests now enter the picture with the approach of the inexorable – death – and even the cure of souls has become, through psychiatry, a secular pursuit. Politics has gone the same route. In China the process is currently passing through a decisive phase as the pragmatics of nation building challenge Mao Zedong's "theologically" vectored Cultural Revolution, but in the West the battle is over. The priest king has gone the way of the medicine man. The claimed discovery (by an Indian astrologer during the heat of the 1964 presidential campaign) that Lyndon Baines Johnson had practiced austerities on the banks of the Ganges in his previous life "staggers belief," as an Indian newspaper commented.

It might seem natural to suppose that (with man's progressive mastery of domains of his existence and the attendant emancipation of these from the custody of religion) the sacred is shrinking and becoming residual, but we should be careful about jumping to that conclusion. It is true that the sacred is less evident in contemporary life than it was in the past, but to this perception three that are less obvious should be added. (1) More of it persists than meets the eye. (2) What remains of it is durable, sufficiently so that it is not likely to decline much further. (3) On the contrary, the sacred is likely to make a comeback – there are signs that it is already doing so.

These are controversial claims, so they require support. I begin with some theoretical considerations and proceed to ones that are a bit more empirical.

If "the secular" defines regions of life that man *controls*, the view that it is displacing the sacred entails the corollary that life is becoming more manageable and (if one carries the view to its logical limit) will eventually become completely manageable. In actuality, however, it is far from clear that man's control over life is increasing. *Parts* of life are coming under control – infectious diseases, infant mortality, and dental hygiene, for example – but it is a far cry from that fact to the conclusion that life as a whole is more under our control.

Item. Human problems tend to be mercurial; solve one and another moves in to take its place. Frequently the new problem is created by the solution to the original one. We wipe out infectious disease and face the population explosion. We solve our energy shortage by splitting the atom, and with precisely that act we are handed the atom bomb and nuclear waste. We invent pesticides, and "silent spring" awaits. Technology used to be considered our servant, but there are ominous signs that it is carrying us to no one knows where. To the extent that this fear is justified, technology dethrones *deus ex machina* to ensconce itself as *deus in machina*, and man remains as much a creature as he was in the former. We are back to the same general problem we faced when we asked about the relation of secularization to the sacred. There it took the form, Does increasing secularization diminish the sacred? Here it reads, does solving life's problems reduce their number or merely change their specifics?

Item. Beyond being unattainable, the idea of complete control isn't even coherent. Man is a social animal and as such lives as one will among others. No one of these wills could become omnipotent without ceasing to be social, for social existence necessarily involves both give and take. This positions "omnipotent" and "social" as logical alternatives.

Finally, not only is the notion of total control contradictory, it isn't even attractive. To enter a friendship, to say nothing of marriage, with intent to control it is to soil the prospect from the start.

Life calls for balancing the rewards of control with gifts that come to us through openness and surrender. The more we resolve to have things our own way, the more closed we become to the virtues in alternative ways. If we cannot perceive the virtue inherent in the capacity to surrender – to surrender to another person in love, or to obligation in the sense of feeling its claims upon us – cynicism awaits us.

These three points relate to our inquiry as follows: Assuming that the sacred lies somewhere within what exceeds human control, there is no reason to think that technology has shrunk that domain. Life continues to dangle over seventy thousand fathoms; only the regions of the deeps have shifted.

Are there new quarters within what we do not control where the sacred might be bidding to show itself today? To sharpen our search we can note that the sacred exceeds not only our control but our comprehension. We can't control the weather, but now that meteorologists have banished the nature gods we no longer find it mysterious.

One candidate is unconscious regions of our minds. By definition, we don't know what goes on there, and clearly we don't control it. "Where id was, let ego be," Freud counseled, and he would have been the first to insist on how far we are from reaching that goal, if indeed it is reachable in principle. To these two features of the unconscious we should now add a third condition of the sacred which the unconscious satisfies: its importance. Recent experimental studies of sleep are reported to reveal that approximately 80 percent of the time male subjects are dreaming they have erections. If the report is accurate, it provides experimental support for what I suspect is true in any case; namely, that the unconscious lies close to the wellsprings of our vitality.

Incomprehensible, indomitable, and important – these are authentic marks of the sacred, and the unconscious possesses them all. Following a lecture my psychologist wife gave at the Graduate Theological Union in Berkeley, the first question she was asked by a theological student was, "Now that we have Jung, do we need religion?" And Ronald Laing, Director of the Langham

Clinic for Psychotherapy in London, argues that in certain cases psychosis is a state of mind in which religious resources of the unconscious can surface with unusual directness. Our unconscious minds hold over us the power of life and death, psychic health and insanity, which is a kind of psychic death, with severe depression falling somewhere in between. We stand in relation to it as creature, a sufficient reason being that (as remarked) it is unfathomable: its thoughts are not our thoughts nor its ways our ways, "our" referring here to what we are in conscious possession of. Human beings are not noticeably open to the divine in any quarter today, but angle for angle, the unconscious provides one continuing locus for its entry. This partly explains the striking impact that Hinduism and Buddhism are having on the West, especially on Western youth, for Asian religious symbolism – "Atman is Brahman," "each of us possesses the Buddha-mind already" – accommodates epiphanies from our unconscious minds more readily than does Judeo-Christian imagery, which tends to picture God as residing outside ourselves.

In addition to the unconscious, there is a second frontier on which the sacred retains its rights in the face of continuing secularization; namely, interpersonal relations, that highly elusive, treacherous, and potentially sublime terrain where two or more persons meet and exchange words and feelings.

The importance of these relations needs no arguing. They create and sustain us, but we have seen that importance by itself doesn't make something sacred. Personal relations have always been important, but in the past they have provided less of an aperture for the divine because they were less problematical. In traditional societies most men and women live their entire lives in a single primary group whose members know one another intimately and for life. Such abiding communities don't prevent unhappiness, but they do spare their members the deeper disturbances that appear when communication breaks down seriously: loneliness, withdrawal, identity confusion, and existential dread.

Thanks to the fact that our society has become impersonal, these maladies are with us. American families now change residence across state lines on the average of once every five years, and wherever they live, they usually work elsewhere. As a consequence they know one another only (a) in stages of life and (b) in aspects of self – in roles, such as husband, professional, customer, voter, client.

These developments have produced in industrial societies a kind of crisis in communication; personal relations, while continuing to be essential, have become precarious as never before. This combination of importance and fragility provides a clearing for the divine, particularly when to those two attributes we add unpredictability and the mystery that attend deep encounters between persons. A perceptive soul like Martin Buber sensed this and wrote a tract for our times, *I and Thou,* which argues that God lives precisely in the intersection of lives at depth level. Encounter groups (T-Groups, Sensitivity Training Groups) provide another evidence that the interpersonal has become an area where the sacred can surface today. Last summer I directed in India a seminar composed of university women, sixteen American and sixteen Indian. The Americans found encounter-group exercises both more threatening and more significant than did the Indians, who (still nurtured by relatively tight and stable primary associations) chattered merrily along as if this were their normal fare. Westerners may like or feel threatened by encounter groups, but almost invariably they find the experience to be different. It also tends to be *important,* for some, the most important experience of their lives. With a dozen or so independent and emotionally charged souls affecting the course of the group, it is unpredictable and *uncontrolled.* And the trajectory of the group *defies comprehension;* there come points when so much is going on, at so many levels, interpreted so divergently by everyone present, that one looks out at the group with eyes of insanity, so totally lacking is anything that approaches an objective grasp of what's happening. All three prerequisites of the sacred are present. It is, therefore, no surprise to find coming from the pen of one of the most practiced leaders of encounter groups an article titled "Sensitivity Training as Religious Experience." When, writes James Clark,

for forty or fifty hours one is confronted in a complex and deeply human way by nearly a dozen other people in a circle with no imposed task to fly into, no hierarchy to bind, contain and ritualize, more often than not one expands. A person experiences the limits he and his environment have imposed on him, and expands beyond them. Knowing what one cannot give, one is able to offer what one can give. And knowing what one can give leads to a sense of where one is in the universe and a genuine experience of the prizing of all men, the mystical, deep, religious, expansive experience of knowing that "no man is an island."

Of an encounter group at Tavistock Institute in England, Margaret Rioch writes: "Everyone, I think, suffered a sea change into something rich and strange, something that borders on the sacred."

In targeting the unconscious and interpersonal regions of human life as two places that are open to the sacred today I have no intention of overlooking or belittling the place one thinks of first, namely churches, synagogues, and their like which came into existence to make room for the sacred. It is, rather, that, driven as they are by crosscurrents of innumerable sorts, institutionalized religions present such a tangled scene today that I have deliberately chosen to exclude them from consideration in this essay. Some day I may address their case, but at this point my thoughts are too unformed and conflicting to be committed to print.

With that proviso in place I turn in the balance of this essay to the regular mode in which the sacred announces itself – revelations – to ask if they are occurring less today than formerly.

Alternatively known as epiphanies or theophanies, revelations are unheralded manifestations that cast things in a different light. As such, they conform to the three marks of the sacred I have been working with: they are not subject to our control, they wear the stamp of importance, and they outstrip our understanding. The genuineness of what they reveal – are they authentic revelations or only subjective inventions? – cannot be objectively determined, and images used to describe them are various. Some recipients report being transported to another, more momentous world, like the man Saint Paul tells of who was transported to the third heaven where he was told things he was not permitted to repeat. Others find messengers from the momentous world turning up in this world as angels. Still others don't speak of other worlds at all, but rather of the pieces of this world being gestalted anew in ways that now make sense.

Revelations can be terrifying, but as conveyers of new gestalts they bring happiness of a sort that differs from the ordinary kind for carrying noetic claims – they ask us to upgrade our estimates of life and the world. The most emphatic epiphanies are those that arrive in times of darkness and despair. The happiness these bring has earned for them a distinctive name, blessedness, the distinctive feature of which is its paradoxical character. Blessedness is paradoxical for shining in darkness that remains visible while light permeates it. To fully comprehend this fact is to find it not just astonishing but astounding; it is an affront to human logic. The peace that comes when we are hungry and find food; when we are lonely and find a friend; when we are sick and feel health returning – these happinesses are understandable. But blessedness is the peace that arrives when these resolutions do not occur. It comes – or can come; there is nothing inevitable about it – when all options are exhausted and life has us by the throat. It could be the death of a child, or an incurable disease, or the onset of blindness. Such things happen, and they make us wish that life were different, that it would approach us in a different guise. But this is the way it has approached us, and we have no choice but to accept its visitation as our identity from that point on.

The question for this essay with its focus on the contemporary scene is whether our secular age is visited less frequently by epiphanies than were former ages, but that they continue to occur is incontrovertible. On my desk is the report of a New York housewife who, in the midst of a deep depression caused by her sister's suicide which left three motherless children, found her depression suddenly lifted and replaced by an inexplicable serenity that embraced rather than eclipsed clear-eyed cognizance of all that had happened. I find such resolutions also in Sidney Cohen's reports of terminal cancer patients who under LSD continue to feel their pain but in a way that no longer matters, so completely is it set in cosmic perspective.

The pain is changed. I know that when I pressed here yesterday, I had an unendurable pain. I couldn't even stand the weight of a blanket. Now I press hard – it hurts, it hurts all right – but it doesn't register as terrifying.

And these:

I could die now, quietly, uncomplaining – like those early Christians in the arena who must have watched the lions eating their entrails.

I see that the hard deaths, too, must be borne. Like difficult births, they are a part of life.

When I die I won't be remembered long – there aren't many friends, and hardly any relatives left. Nothing much accomplished – no children, nothing. But that's all right too.

Several swallows don't make a spring, of course, and I know of no way to move from spot-checks like the ones given to statistical conclusions about our times. In his empirical studies of peak experiences, Abraham Maslow found both that such experiences are virtually universal – almost all his subjects reported having had them – and that to an extent that surprised him as an investigator, they tended to characterize them as religious in their character and feel. But what are we to make of that finding?

Despairing of arriving at a quantitative conclusion, I will fall back on surmises, which begin by noting that revelations have two poles: a sender (whether personified as God, or limited to the state-of-affairs that is disclosed) and a receiver. Secular modes of thought could handicap receivers today, causing them to discount intimations they might otherwise take seriously, but there is another way to view the matter, and I will devote the remainder of this essay to sketching it.

If man is in fact a theomorphic being, as the historical religions all claim, the image of God is the most important fact about us. It stands to reason that this component will not submit without resistance to being caged in a secular outlook. If it actually exists, it will be like a jack-in-the-box, the spring of which constantly pressures the lid to open and let it out.

I am impressed by the evidence I see that supports this view of the self. Equating secularism with skepticism, we think of ours as a skeptical age, but I have come to question the equation. With New Age credulities busting out all over, our scientific, high-tech, and in ways secular age may turn out in fact to be one of the most believing ages in history. The objects of belief have changed, but faith remains securely in place.

Item. Last year while teaching for a quarter at Santa Barbara, I was invited to the home of a family I had chanced to know in Mexico several years earlier. In the course of the evening it developed that a visiting sister was completely wrapped up in the Los Angeles chapter of Maharishi Mahesh Yogi's International Meditation Society, while the high-school-sophomore daughter was a moving spirit of the local chapter of the Sokagakai chanting sect. Driving home I stopped for gasoline and found the filling station attendant completing D. T. Suzuki's *Zen Buddhism*. In a single evening I had met six persons, three of whom were involved – two very deeply – with religion in forms that elude the usual opinion polls.

Item. Lest the preceding episode be discounted on grounds that it is precisely what one might expect in California, I choose my next one from staid New England. Two years ago a group of eight M.I.T. upperclassmen formed a preceptoral group and asked me to be their instructor. It was to be an independent study project which the students were to conduct themselves, my role being limited to that of adviser and consultant. Ostensibly on Asian thought, it began respectably enough with standard Chinese and Indian texts, but as the weeks moved on and the students' true interests surfaced, the original syllabus began to lurch and reel until I found myself holding on to my mortarboard wondering whether to continue in the role of sober professor or turn anthropologist, sit back, and observe the ways of the natives. For natives in thought-patterns they were; far closer to Hottentots than to scientific positivists. In the end the anthropologist in me triumphed over the academician, for I found the window to this strange and (in the technical, anthropological sense) quite primitive mentality fascinating. I cannot recall the exact progression of topics, but it went something like this: Beginning with Asian philosophy, it moved on to meditation, then yoga, then Zen, then Tibet, then successively to the *Bardo Thodol,* tantra, the kundalini, the chakras, the *I Ching,* karate and aikido, the yin-yang macrobiotic (brown rice) diet, Gurdjieff, Meher Baba, astrology, astral bodies, auras, UFOs, Tarot cards, parapsychology, witchcraft, and magic. And, underlying everything, of course, the psychedelic drugs. The students weren't dallying with these matters. They were *on* the drugs; they were *eating* brown rice; they were meditating hours on end; they were making their decisions by the *I Ching,* which one student considered the most important discovery of his life; they were constructing electronic experiments to prove that their thoughts, via psychokinesis, could affect matter directly.

And they weren't plebeians, Haight-Ashbury flower children. Intellectually they were aristocrats with the highest math scores in the land, Ivy League verbal scores, and two to three years of saturation in M.I.T. science. What *they* learned in the course of the semester I have no way of knowing. What I learned was that the human mind stands ready to believe anything – absolutely anything – as long as it offers an alternative to the desecularized mechanomorphic outlook of objective science. Some may see the lesson as teaching no more than the extent of human credulity, but I read the matter differently. If mechanomorphism is the truth, then indeed the students' gropings reveal no more than human unwillingness to accept its strictures. But if reality *is* in fact sacred, the students' frenetic thrusts suggest something different. In matters of spirit, subject and object mesh exceptionally – no faith, no God; no response, no revelation. It follows that the sacred depends heavily on man's nose for it. Given noses as keen for the chase as my students' were, if the sacred lingers anywhere in the interstices of contemporary life, it is going to be flushed out.

Item. Credulity isn't confined to the young. Returning recently by plane from Chicago to Boston I found myself seated next to a physics professor. She discussed physics with interest, but flying saucers with passion – passionate belief. UFOs are not, to be sure, ideal exemplars of the sacred, but they impinge on it by virtue of awakening numinous feelings, for if they should exist, they are probably manned by creatures more advanced than we. So they do more than puzzle. They are strange.

Item. Turning from personal anecdotes to the world at large: that Japan is the most literate nation in the world, and the most industrialized in Asia, has not prevented more than five hundred new religions from springing up there since World War II.

Item. Science fiction is booming. Only in part does space exploration account for this; we can as readily turn the matter around and say that the will to transcend the mundane has fueled space exploration. In the past this will, working on the imagination, produced the "Gothic" novel with its preternatural incursions. It also produced spiritualism and its interest in phenomena that are neither clearly natural nor clearly supernatural. Today science fiction, especially where located in space as in *Star Wars,* accomplishes the same imaginative transcendence by envisioning encounters with natural but transterrestrial beings. Mythological and psychological supernaturalism are replaced by a transterrestrial and uncanny naturalism.

To conclude: the polarity of the sacred and the secular continues to hold its place among the mighty opposites that crisscross life: systole and diastole, action and repose, freedom and form, centrifugal and centripetal, yang and yin. If man is in fact *homo religiosus,* he is by nature vulnerable to transcendental visitations – susceptible to intimations of Otherness at the thin places that separate us from an encompassing More. By this reading, when 57 percent of the American public say that religion is losing its influence, they should be saying that institutionalized religion is losing its influence in certain areas of life where its presence used to be more evident. But as institutionalized religion isn't the whole of religion, the fact that the sacred has withdrawn from certain spheres does not prove that as a free-floating phenomenon it is diminishing. Robert Bellah could be right in detecting in the United States at the moment something of a religious revival.

Thinking Allowed with Jeffrey Mishlove:
A Televised Interview

I *tack on this second appendix as a kind of coda to provide an idea as to how the thoughts that this book has ranged through might be summarized for a general audience. It consists of the edited transcript of Jeffrey Mishlove's 1998 interview with me in his television series, "Thinking Allowed."*

JEFFREY MISHLOVE

Hello and welcome. Our topic this evening is the psychology of religious experience, and my guest tonight is one of America's scholars of religious traditions, Dr. Huston Smith. Dr. Smith is a former professor of philosophy at M.I.T. He's the author of a classic study, *The World's Religions,* which has sold over two million copies, as well as eight other books on philosophy, religion, and psychology, most recently one called *Beyond the Post-Modern Mind.* Welcome, Dr. Smith.

HUSTON SMITH

Thank you. It's good to be here.

MISHLOVE

It's a pleasure to have you here. Your background in philosophy, psychology, and religious studies is extensive, and the topic that we're going to discuss – the psychology of religious experience – is broad: there are innumerable religions and they are very diverse. And yet ultimately they all seem to reflect the human mind. Would you say that being a scholar of religions has made you a more religious person yourself?

SMITH

I certainly don't feel that I've become less religious, and I also feel that my studies have deepened and broadened my – what? – my beliefs. In that sense I guess one might say that my studies have made me more religious. I might prefer to say that they have matured me religiously, for my religious bent dates back as far as I can remember.

MISHLOVE

I suppose it's always a little delicate for a scholar, who is supposed to be objective, to study something as intense and passionate as religion can be.

SMITH

Well, some see it as a problem, but I've been fortunate in that I have never felt I had to choose between passion and objectivity. Quite the opposite. Not to have the two conjoined puts you at a disadvantage, it seems to me, for if you are studying something you are not in love with, what are your chances of getting deeply into it and seeing it from inside? It has been my good fortune to have been able to devote my life's work to dealing with what I most love.

MISHLOVE

My first encounter with the psychology of religion in a deep and personal way came from reading William James's classic, *The Varieties of Religious Experience* . . .

SMITH

. . . a wonderful book . . .

MISHLOVE

. . . in which he described his experiments with nitrous oxide and other then-known drugs.

SMITH

That was an adventuresome, courageous move and fully in character with the man that he was.

MISHLOVE

Then in the mid-sixties, I read a book by Timothy Leary and Ralph Metzner called *The Psychedelic Experience*, in which they attempted to create the analogy between the pantheon of gods in the

Hindu and Buddhist traditions and the dynamic forces working in the subconscious mind.

SMITH

Again, a venturesome hypothesis. But it seems to have stood up. There does seem to be a correlation between chemically induced paranormal experiences and spontaneous ones such as those that produced traditional pantheons.

MISHLOVE

An overlap, at least.

SMITH

A marked overlap. We can trace the religious use of mind-altering substances back at least three thousand years, and we now know a good deal about how the brain processes them.

MISHLOVE

You were involved in some of the early work on the connection.

SMITH

Close to the eye of the cyclone, actually. Those were the 1960s. I was teaching at M.I.T. and acted in effect as Aldous Huxley's social secretary during the semester he was with us as a visiting professor. He had published *The Doors of Perception*, which opened the public's eyes to the visionary possibilities of the entheogens. It turned out that Huxley's M.I.T. semester coincided with the fall that Timothy Leary moved from Berkeley to Harvard by way of a summer vacation in Mexico where, on the side of a swimming pool in Cuernavaca, he ingested a handful of psychoactive mushrooms that opened up his mind in ways that took him completely by surprise.

MISHLOVE

Psilocybin mushrooms, I presume.

SMITH

Yes. He had a three-year research appointment at Harvard's Center for Personality Study where he could name his own project, and he decided to see if the dramatic experiences that entheogens can produce have the capacity to change behavior. He had read Huxley's book and drew Huxley into his project as an adviser, and I got drawn in through Huxley.

MISHLOVE

At that time the drugs being studied were perfectly legal.

SMITH

Not only legal; they were respectable – this was officially authorized research at the top university of the land. The first thing that Leary did was to mount an open-ended study in which people would simply describe their experiences under the drugs, and he found that a large proportion of the descriptions had a mystical cast to them. That was the finding that interested me most.

MISHLOVE

You had been studying mysticism long before this, I presume.

SMITH

A fair statement.

MISHLOVE

Had you thought about the relationship between mysticism and drugs prior to your encounters with Leary and Huxley?

SMITH

Academically I had. I had read Huxley's *Doors of Perception,* and his contention that phenomenologically, which is to say descriptively, drug-occasioned visionary experiences are indistinguishable from ones that occur naturally. I conducted an experiment on that point in which I took accounts of classic mystical experiences and intermingled them with descriptions that Leary's subjects provided and asked knowledgeable judges to separate them into their original piles. They were unable to do so.

MISHLOVE

From the accounts they gave, your judges couldn't separate the classical mystics from Leary's subjects.

SMITH

Exactly. Their guesses didn't pan out.

MISHLOVE

That sounds similar to a study Lawrence LeShan conducted. He took statements of mystics and statements of physicists and compared them, and they too seemed almost indistinguishable.

SMITH

That's interesting and pertinent as well, but I won't go into how. The two cases are strikingly similar. But I think it's important to add another point. The evidence I cited shows only that drug and non-drug mystical *experiences* are alike while mysticism includes much more than mystical experiences. Its real concern is with mystical lives, including the compassion and other virtues such lives embody. It think it was Robert Ornstein who put this point graphically when he said that the object of mysticism is not altered states but altered traits. Experiences come and go, whereas it is life's sustained quality that counts. So we have to ask not only whether mystical experiences feel the same but also whether their impact on the lives of their subjects is the same.

MISHLOVE

Good point. And now that we have a twenty-year perspective on the original experiments you refer to, I think it's quite obvious that psychedelic cults don't have the staying power of authentic religious traditions.

What about Leary's claim in *The Psychedelic Experience* that the gods that people tend to project onto the world actually exist inside us, as parts of our own psyches? He seems to have been saying that the pantheons of the ancient pantheistic religions are forces that actually exist, but exist within us. I think he would hold that the same principle holds for monotheisms.

SMITH

We live in a psychological rather than a metaphysical age, and I see no harm in putting things the way you attribute to Tim. Whether we go the psychological or the metaphysical route is a fielder's choice because the important points can be stated either way. We have that option because geography doesn't apply to things of the spirit which elude spatial matrices. The spatial imagery that we attach to spirit is metaphorical only, and not literally accurate. It follows that the distinction between out there and in here, which in everyday life holds categorically, is relativized when religious objects are at issue.

If I can carry the issue one step further, it's natural to position values (good and evil, better and worse) on a vertical axis – superior and inferior, thumbs up, thumbs down.

MISHLOVE

Heaven?

SMITH

Yes. All peoples position their heavens above them and their hells in the bowels of the earth. Gods invariably dwell on mountaintops, and angels sing on high. But we need to add still another point. When we talk about the external world, good is imaged as up and bad as down. But when we introspect and attend to what's inside us, that reversal of attention causes the vertical (value) axis to invert as well. Deep and profound thoughts are better than superficial ones, and a fundamental truth is more important than a shallow one that only skims the surface. I say these things to support my point that the distinction you brought up – between out there and in here – cannot be taken literally when speaking of spiritual matters. It is relative and hence negotiable. Traditionally it was customary to think of God as out there, but in our psychological age there is a move in the direction you pointed to – to think of him/her/it (the pronouns never work) as within ourselves.

MISHLOVE

Another related notion, I think, is the one originally developed by Durkheim, the French sociologist, in which he suggests that religions are really reifications of society's group mind or collective consciousness. God, he argued, is actually a personification of a society's shared values. That sounds like Jung's collective unconscious to me.

SMITH

I can understand why you say that. I find both Durkheim and Jung's hypotheses useful when they are not pushed to their limits.

For one thing, both oppose the all-too-common notion that the mind is reducible to the brain, and therefore (so this reasoning goes) since the brain can be positioned, the mind can be located too. But I remember in a weekend conference in Tucson some years ago where Gregory Bateson asked the psychologists present – people like Carl Rogers and Rollo May – where their minds were located. His question took us aback, but when we saw what he was getting at, we saw it as a deft way of making his point, which was that it's wrong to think that our minds are located in our heads. That's where our brains are, but our minds are at large.

MISHLOVE

And of course we can always go back to the argument of Bishop Berkeley that the entire physical universe, that everything we experience – pots and pans and TV sets – exist only in your mind.

SMITH

Yes, though in fairness to Berkeley, we have to add that the durability of the physical universe derives from the fact that its contents reside in God's mind as well as ours. Otherwise the world would depend on human beings and vanish if human beings became extinct.

MISHLOVE

Right. A needed amendment.

SMITH

We've gotten into ecology here. Everybody's concerned about the ecology of nature, what about the ecology of mind? We're just beginning to get used to that idea, yet it's a daily experience. You can walk into the room and (in current terminology) feel vibrations. We can sense what feels like a wall of anger and hostility, and also sense an ambience of peace. And of course with the move toward field theory, physics too is becoming profoundly ecological. Dig deep enough and we see that what present themselves to us as free-standing, independent objects actually float on webs of relationships. Networking is the way the world works.

MISHLOVE

Picking up on the God within, or "the beyond within" as you title the section on Atman in your chapter on Hinduism, I notice in contemporary religions, particularly in evangelical Christianity, a resistance to God-within language. I assume that they are afraid of self-deification – usurping God's position. How do you feel about that?

SMITH

They have a point and you nailed it. I mean, if someone comes along and says, "I am God," it's perfectly reasonable to counter, "Well, your behavior doesn't seem to bear that out." God by definition is perfect, and what human being can make that claim? So I think the teachers that you refer to have a valid point, but it doesn't annul the concept of the divine within, which remains in place. Hinduism has been the most emphatic of the religions in saying that in the final analysis Atman is Brahman. That translates into saying that the deepest component of the human self is divine. But they accommodate the point you've raised with an analogy. A lantern can be coated with dust, and dirt, and finally caked with mud to the point where the light within it is totally concealed. So both sides of the matter are true. We are indeed divine in essence, but that essence is so clouded with human frailties that it is only marginally detectable.

MISHLOVE

In a previous program you told us about some of your experiences with primal peoples, such as the aborigines in Australia. As I recall your accounts, such peoples can access the divine quite regularly.

SMITH

I think that's so. The aborigines distinguish between our everyday world and what they call the Dreaming. The Dreaming is a transcendent state, or place, wherein the living participate in the lives of their ancestors, and indeed the creation of the world. I suppose we might call it a trancelike state, but they can be in it while going about their daily routines. There's another way in which they're in touch with a transcendent reality or state, and this has to do with parapsychology as we know the word – telepathy, specifically. I was in Australia for a summer (their winter) lecturing at its universities, and I spent my free time with the aborigines and the anthropologists who study them. Those anthropologists were unanimous in believing that the aborigines have telepathic powers. They told me story after story of cases when on a walkabout someone would suddenly announce that someone back home had fallen ill or died. They would retrace their steps, and invariably (according to the anthropologists' reports) the intuition would be validated.

MISHLOVE

That's a strong statement coming from anthropologists, who tend to be quite skeptical.

SMITH

Quite so. Their theory, or presumption, was that these are normal human powers, but like any power it can atrophy if it is not used. It can also be blocked if our conceptual mind disbelieves it.

MISHLOVE

Do you see some religious traditions encouraging the cultivation of psychic capacities more than others do?

SMITH

Well, it's interesting. I'll put it slightly differently. Most religions believe that paranormal powers exist – *siddis*, the Indians call them . . .

MISHLOVE

. . . meaning powers? . . .

SMITH

. . . yes, and that they tend to increase as one advances spiritually. However, religions tend to treat them gingerly. If you make their acquisition your goal you are settling for too little, and if you master some of them your wonder-workings can breed spiritual pride. Also, the domain is treacherous, so if you don't have a competent teacher you can go off the deep end. So authentic teachers tend to acknowledge the *siddis* while advising that we not get caught up in them.

MISHLOVE

But aren't there traditions – the shamanistic traditions in particular – that place great importance in these powers?

SMITH

Actually, in various ways all traditions do. To pick up on the shamans that you mention, the Mayans call them "spirit-lawyers," that is, men or women who go to the spirits and try to argue them into giving benefits of various sorts to human beings. They perform valuable services for their communities, but one doesn't associate sanctity with shamans.

MISHLOVE

Well, as our program winds up, I wonder if there's a message that you would like to leave with our viewers this evening? Something you might pass on to them from your studies?

SMITH

Let's see. Let me try this:

Religious institutions, though they are indispensable, are a mixed bag, but the basic claim that they put forward is true. And what that claim asserts – I'm paraphrasing William James here – is that the best things are the eternal things, the things in the universe that throw the last stone, so to speak, and say the final word.

NOTES AND REFERENCES

Chapter 2

1. A. R. Vidler, ed., *Soundings: Essays Concerning Christian Understandings* (Cambridge: Cambridge University Press, 1962). The statement cited appears on page 72, in H. A. Williams's essay "Theology and Self-Awareness."

2. Edith Hamilton, *Mythology* (New York: Mentor, 1953), p. 55.

3. Quoted in Alan Watts, *The Spirit of Zen* (New York: Grove Press, 1958), p. 110.

4. George Mylonas, *Eleusis and the Eleusinian Mysteries* (Princeton, NJ: Princeton University Press, 1961), p. 284.

5. Henri Bergson, *Two Sources of Morality and Religion* (New York: Holt, 1935), pp. 206–12.

6. Mary Barnard, "The God in the Flowerpot," *The American Scholar* 32, 4 (Autumn 1963): 584, 586.

7. R. C. Zaehner, *Mysticism, Sacred and Profane* (New York: Oxford University Press, 1961), p. 12.

8. Quoted in William H. McGlothlin, "Long-Lasting Effects of LSD on Certain Attitudes in Normals," printed for private distribution by the RAND Corporation (May 1962), p. 16.

9. Ibid., pp. 45, 46.

10. Timothy Leary, "The Religious Experience: Its Production and Interpretation," *The Psychedelic Review* 1, 3 (1964): 325.

11. Walter N. Pahnke, "Drugs and Mysticism: An Analysis of the Relationship Between Psychedelic Drugs and the Mystical Consciousness," a thesis presented to the Committee on Higher Degrees in History and Philosophy of Religion, Harvard University (June 1963).

12. The first account is quoted anonymously in "The Issue of the Consciousness-Expanding Drugs," *Main Currents in Modern Thought* 20, 1 (September–October 1963): 10–11. The second experience was that of Dr. R. M. Bucke, the author of *Cosmic Consciousness*, as quoted in William James, *The Varieties of Religious Experience* (New York: Modern

Library, 1902), pp. 290–91. The former experience occurred under the influence of drugs; the latter did not.

13. James S. Slotkin, *Peyote Religion* (New York: Free Press of Glencoe, 1956).

14. G. M. Carstairs, "Daru and Bhang," *Quarterly Journal of the Study of Alcohol* 15 (1954): 229.

15. Michael Polanyi, *Personal Knowledge* (Chicago: University of Chicago Press, 1958).

16. Sigmund Freud, *Totem and Taboo* (New York: Modern Library, 1938).

17. William James, *The Varieties of Religious Experience* (1902; reprint ed., New York: Macmillan Publishing Company, 1961), pp. 305–6.

18. "The Hallucinogenic Fungi of Mexico: An Inquiry into the Origins of the Religious Idea Among Primitive Peoples," *Harvard Botanical Museum Leaflets* 19, 7 (1961).

19. Margaret Prescott Montague, *Twenty Minutes of Reality* (St. Paul, MN: Macalester Park, 1947), pp. 15, 17.

20. "The Current Scientific Status of Psychedelic Drug Research," read at the Conference on Methods in Philosophy and the Sciences, New School for Social Research, 3 May 1964.

21. Quoted by Dr. Sanford M. Unger in the paper just mentioned.

22. Albert Camus, *The Myth of Sisyphus* (New York: Vintage, 1955), p. 38.

23. William James, *op. cit.*, p. 379.

24. From an early draft of a manuscript by Philip Kapleau that was published as *The Three Pillars of Zen* (Boston: Beacon Press, 1967).

25. Slotkin, *op. cit.*

Chapter 3

1. Quoted in *A Zen Forest: Sayings of the Masters*, trans. Soiku Sigematsu (New York: Weatherhill, 1981).

Chapter 4

1. R Gordon Wasson, *SOMA: Divine Mushroom of Immortality*, Ethnomycological Studies, no. 1 (New York: Harcourt Brace Jovanovich, 1968, 1971).

2. I have not been able to find the statement in his writings, but I am confident of my memory. Frithjof Schuon says of the Vedanta that it "appears among explicit doctrines as one of the most direct formulations possible of that which makes the very essence of our spiritual reality" (*Spiritual Perspectives and Human Facts*, p. 95).

3. Recounted in his book co-authored with the greatest living mycologist, Roger Heim.

4. "Fly" from the fact that the mushroom attracts flies and sends them temporarily into a stupor (Europeans used it as a flycatcher until quite recently); "agaric" from an error in classification. When Linnaeus came to mushrooms he found the whole domain so frustratingly complicated that he grew careless and used "agarikon," which is actually a tree fungus, to designate the gilled, fleshy-capped mushrooms.

Publications by R. Gordon Wasson Cited in the Text

1. "The Hallucinogenic Fungi of Mexico: An Inquiry Into the Origins of the Religious Idea Among Primitive Peoples," *Botanical Museum Leaflets* (Harvard University) XIX, 7 (1961).

2. With Roger Heim, *Les Champignons Hallucinogenes du Mexique* (Paris: Archives du Museum National d'Histoire Naturelle), Serie 7, Tome VI, 1958 (1959).

3. With Valentina Pavlovna Wasson, *Mushrooms, Russia and History*, 2 vols. (New York: Pantheon Books, 1957).

4. *SOMA, Divine Mushroom of Immortality* (New York: Harcourt Brace Jovanovich, 1968, 1971).

5. "*SOMA:* Comments Inspired by Professor Kuiper's Review," *Indo-Iranian Journal* XII, 4 (1970).

6. "*SOMA:* Mr. Wasson's Rejoinder to Professor Brough," in press as a monograph to be published by the Botanical Museum of Harvard University. Page numbers are those in the typescript.

7. "The Soma of the Rig-Veda: What Was It?" *Journal of the American Oriental Society* XCI, 2 (April–June 1971).

Reviews of Wasson's SOMA in English, French, and German

8. Andre Bareau, in *Journal Asiatique* (1969): 173–76.

9. G. Becker, in *Revue de Mycologie* XXXIV, 1 (1969): 84–87.

10. John Brough, "Soma and Amanita muscaria," *Bulletin of the School of Oriental and African Studies* (University of London) XXXIV, 2 (1971).

11. P. Demieville, in *T'oung Pao* LVI, 4–5: 298–302.

12. Robert Graves, "The Divine Rite of Mushrooms," *Atlantic Monthly* (February 1970): 109–13.

13. Catherine R. and Kate Hammond, "The Mystery of Soma," *Sunday Herald Traveler* 2 (August 1971), Book Section, pp. 1–2.

14. Daniel Ingalls, "Remarks on Mr. Wasson's Soma," *Journal of the America Oriental Society* XCI, 2 (April–June 1971): 188–91.

15. Daniel Ingalls, in *The New York Times Book Review* (5 September 1971), p. 15.

16. Jacques Kayaloff, in *The Russian Review* (April 1970): 233–39.

17. Stella Kiamrisch, forthcoming in *Artibus Asiae*.

18. F. B. J. Kuiper, in *Indo-Iranian Journal* XII, 4 (1970): 279–85. Rejoinder by R. Gordon Wasson, pp. 286–98.

19. Weston La Barre, in *American Anthropologist* LXXII (March 1970): 368–71.

20. Claude Lévi-Strauss, "Les Champignons dans la Culture: A propos d'un livre de M. R. G. Wasson," *L'Homme* X (1970): 5–16.

21. Portions of the above, translated by Alfred Corn, "Claude Lévi-Strauss: Mushrooms in Culture," *University Review* 12 (1970), unpaged.

22. B. Lowy, in *Review Mycologia* LXI, 4 (July–August 1969): 849–51.

23. M. M. Payak, in *Indian Phytopathology* XXII, 4 (December 1969): 527–30.

24. A. Pilat, in *Schweizerische Zeitschrift für Pilzkunde: Bulletin Suisse de Mycologie* XLVIII (November 1970): 133–43.

25. Winthrop Sargent, "Mainstay of the Sky, Foundation of the Earth," *The New Yorker* (30 May 1970): 90ff.

26. Richard Evans Schultes, in *Economic Botany* XXV, 1 (January–March 1971): 111–12.

27. Richard Evans Schultes, in *Journal of Psychedelic Drugs* III, 2 (September 1971): 104–5.

28. Michael Sullivan, in *Journal of the American Oriental Society* XCI, 2 (1971): 346.

29. Unsigned, "Ariadne," *New Scientist* (3 September 1970): 494.

30. Unsigned, "Daily Closeup," *New York Post* (19 August 1971).

31. Unsigned, in *Times Literary Supplement* (22 May 1969). Correspondence: 21 August 1970; 11 September 1970; 25 September 1970.

32. S. Henry Wassen, in *Saertryk af Friesia* (Copenhagen) 330–32, and in *Svenska Dagbladet* (8 August 1969).

Chapter 5

1. Irmgard Schloegl, *The Wisdom of the Zen Masters* (New York: New Directions, 1975), p. 21.
2. A. K. Coomaraswamy, *Hinduism and Buddhism* (New York: The Philosophical Library, 1943), p. 30.

Chapter 6

1. The flyleaf of Rank's book which served as almost the bible for Grof's work in one of its stages carries a quotation from Nietzsche: "The very best . . . is, not to be born. . . . The next best . . . is . . . to die soon."
2. Dr. Grof's studies did not stop a quarter century ago when the foregoing report of it was written. His recently published book, *The Cosmic Game: Explorations of the Frontiers of Human Consciousness* (Albany, NY: State University of New York Press, 1998), picks up the story where it leaves off here.

Chapter 7

W. N. Pahnke, "Drugs and Mysticism: An Analysis of the Relationship Between Psychedelic Drugs and the Mystical Consciousness." Unpublished doctoral dissertation, Harvard University, Cambridge, 1963. Summarized in W. N. Pahnke, "Drugs and Mysticism," *The International Journal of Parapsychology* 8, no. 2 (1966): 295–320.

R. Doblin, "Pahnke's 'Good Friday Experiment': A Long-Term Follow-Up and Methodological Critique," *The Journal of Transpersonal Psychology* 23, no. 1 (1990): 1–28.

Chapter 8

Hillary Jenkins, *Newman's Mediterranean Voyage* (Dublin: Irish University Press, 1974).

D. H. Salman and R. H. Prince, eds., *Do Psychedelics Have Religious Implications?* (Montreal: McGill University/R. M. Bucke Society, 1967), pp. 1–12.

INDEX

A

aborigines, 18, 156–57
abreaction, 84
Absolute, the, 6, 96
acedia, 75
actualization, supreme, 69
afterlife, 19, 47n
Agni, 47n, 48–49
alcohol, 20
alcoholics, 34, 124
Alcoholics Anonymous, founding of, 129
Alexander, George, 10, 11, 13
Algonquin Indians, 47n
Amanita muscaria, 55, 57–60
anesthesia, 25, 71
antinomianism, 39–41
apocalypticism, 38
archetypes, 92
artificial intelligence, 35–36
atman, 70, 71, 156
aversion. *See* Poisons, Three
awareness, 70, 75n

B

Barnard, Mary, 19, 47n
Barron, Frank, 10
Bateson, Gregory, 155
Bear, Beatrice Weasel, 119
beauty and harmony, 12n, 110n
Becker, Jeffrey, 74n
Bellah, Robert, 135, 147
Bellow, Saul, 68, 69, 114
Berkeley, Bishop, 155

Beyond Health and Normality (Walsh and Shapiro), 65, 68–69, 72
Beyond the Post-Modern Mind (Smith), 149
Bhagavad Gita, 42
bhakti, 24
bhang, 24
Bible, 19–20, 37, 117
Bieberman, Lisa, 16
Big Bang, 65–66
Big Picture, 3
birth, giving
    peyote and, 125
birth process, 89. *See also* trauma, of birth
    stages in, 88, 89
Blackbird, Ethel, 124
Blake, William, 74, 75
bliss, 70, 95. *See also* ecstasy; joyousness
body(ies), 71, 91, 92
    physical, 93, 96
boundaries, ego, 75n
Brahman, 70, 72, 156
Brahmins, 63
Brämanas, 49
Brough, John, 60
Brown, Daniel, 74
Buber, Martin, 140
Buddha, 1, 63
Buddhism, 75, 139, 151
    Zen, 6, 18, 30–31, 40–42, 74, 144
Buddhism in China (Ch'en), 41
Buddhist doctrine of Six Realms of Existence, 130–31

C

Camus, Albert, 29
Carstairs, G. M., 24
Catholicism, 24, 77, 111
causal body, 71, 92, 93
cells, 96
certainty, absolute, 22, 23, 34, 35
Ch'an/Zen tradition, 41, 42
charismatic leaders, 36–37
Ch'en, Kenneth, 41
China, 1, 2, 41
Chirico, Georgio de, 2
Christ, 23, 39, 87, 101. See also Jesus
Christianity, 37–38, 41–42. See also
        Catholicism; Protestantism
churches, 15–16, 36. See also specific
        churches and religions
Clark, James, 140–41
Clark, Walter Houston, 16, 100
Cohen, Sidney, 142
colors. See visions and visual
        experiences
Compton, Arthur, 131–32
consciousness
    cosmic, 92
    five bands of, 11
    relation between brain activity and,
        66–67
    states/forms of, 26–27, 70, 95–96
        ordinary/waking, IX, 27, 70
"contractual daylight" model of self,
        68, 69
control, things beyond human, 138
Cook, Loretta Afraid-of-Bear, 123, 125
Coomaraswamy, A. K., 77–78
Council on Spiritual Practices, xv
Creator, 116–18. See also God
criminals. See lawbreakers

D

Dailey, Truman, 117, 122
Daumal, René, 34
death, 68, 87, 89

and bereavement, 125
    fear of, 76
death experiences, 86, 87
defense systems, 90
delusions, 28
demi-gods, 130–31
Dependent Origination, Formulation
        of, 89–90
depression, 142
desire. See Poisons, Three
discipline, 31, 42
Doblin, Rick, 104
Doors of Perception, The (Huxley), xv,
        6, 17, 20, 23, 63, 151, 152
Dostoevsky, Fyodor, 107, 109n
Dreaming, 156
dreams, 70, 82, 138
drug addiction, alleviated by
        entheogens, 123–24
drug experiences. See also specific
        drugs; specific topics
    fearful, 10, 27, 127–30
    life-changing, 129, 142
    reasons for doubting the
        authenticity of, 23–25
    reports/descriptions of, 22–23
        Smith's, 10–13, 100–103
drugs. See also specific drugs; specific
        topics
    capacity to change behavior, 123–24,
        129
    effects on brain, 29
    fascination vs. fear of, 54
    forbidden by Buddha, 63
    "half-life," 63
    research on, 9. See also Grof, Stanislav;
        Harvard Project; LSD therapy
        double-blind, 21–22
Dukkha, 1
Durkheim, Émile, 154

E

Eckhart, Meister, 73

ecstasy, VIII, 27, 28, 49, 52, 92. *See also*
  bliss; joyousness
Ecstatic Adventure, The (Metzner), 15,
  46n
ego. *See also* self
  development of sense of, 74n
ego-dissolution, 75
ego-transcendence, 36, 78
Eleusinian Mysteries, 18, 113, 115
emanation theory, 11, 46n
emanationism, 11
empathy, 87
empirical metaphysics, 11, 46n
"Empirical Metaphysics" (Smith), 46n
encounter groups, 140–41
enlightenment, 31
entheogens. *See also* drugs
  meaning, XVI–XVII
Ephesians, 20
essence, 156
essence-accident metaphysics, 26
Etsitty, Larry, 119
evil, rescinded, 87, 124
existential crisis, 85–87
"existentials," 92

F

faith, 31
fear, 54, 76
  drug-induced experiences of, 11,
    130. *See also* drug experiences,
    negative
Findlay, J. N., 41n
fire, 22, 48–49, 131
fly agaric. *See Amanita muscaria*
Forgotten Truth (Smith), XVI, 79, 80, 89,
  91, 95
free associations, 67–68
Freud, Sigmund, 25, 69, 97, 138
Freudian model, 35, 36, 82, 84, 85, 89.
  See also psychoanalysis
Frost, Robert, 133
fusion. *See* union

G

Gap, Eva, 125
God, 5, 92, 95, 104–5, 139
  awareness of and experiencing, 6,
    12, 21, 23–24, 100–101, 118. *See
    also* theophanies
  concept of, 97
  entheogens and, 80
  identification with, 156
  loving and being loved by, 105, 116
  self-disclosure of, 65
godlessness, 114, 115
gods, pantheon of, 45–50, 46n, 150–51,
  153
Good Friday Experiment, 99–105
Graves, Robert, 53, 59
Great Chain of Being, XVI, 4
Great Spirit, 119–21
  hearing the voice of the, 23
Grof, Stanislav, 80–97
gross body, 71

H

hallucination. *See also* visions and
    visual experiences
  defined, XVI
happiness, 23, 76–77. *See also*
    joyousness
Harvard Project, 15–16
Heard, Gerald, 4–6
Heim, Roger, 51
Heisenberg, Werner, 132
Hensley, Albert, 117
Hinduism, 139, 151, 156. *See also*
    Vedanta
Hofmann, Albert, VIII, XV, XVI, 33, 115,
  133
human beings and humanity. *See also*
    specific topics
  modernity's vs. traditional cultures'
    view of, 69
  as multilayered, 82

Hunter, Lawrence, 125
Huxley, Aldous, VIII, XV, XVII, 5–7, 23,
    151, 152

I

I Ching, 145
Ice, Bernard, 119
Idiot, The (Dostoevsky), 109n
ignorance. *See* Poisons, Three
immortality, 49. *See also* afterlife
India, 62, 63, 67, 70, 140
Indian philosophy, 70
Indra, 48, 60
infinite, 2, 75, 97
    entheogens and, 80
Ingalls, Daniel, 47n, 49, 53, 58
insights, 22, 92. *See also* revelations
    conviction that they are true, 34, 35.
    See also certainty
International Federation for Internal
    Freedom, 16
interpersonal relations, 139

J

Jakobson, Roman, 60
James, William, IX, XV, 26, 30, 35, 150, 158
Janiger, Oscar, 21
Japan, 146
Jenkins, Hillary, 108
Jesse, Robert, 99
Jesus, 114, 115. *See also* Christ
jivamukta, 75, 77
John, Peter, 16
Johnson, Lyndon Baines, 136
joriki, 31
joyousness, 22, 28, 76. *See also* bliss;
    ecstasy
Jung, Carl G., 86, 154

K

Katha Upanisad, 42

kensho, 31
Kipling, Rudyard, 75
Kleps, Arthur, 36
knowledge
    secret religious, 41–43, 80
    tacit, 67
Kochampanaskin, Ralph, 120
Kozad, Andy, 124
Kramrisch, Stella, 58
Krishna, 42
Kuniper, F. B. J., 57–58

L

La Barre, Weston, 59
Laing, Ronald D., 138–39
Lallemand, Charles, 47n
lawbreakers, 34
Leary, Timothy, 6, 10–12, 17, 33, 36,
    151–53
Lee, Paul, 16
LeShan, Lawrence, 153
Lévi-Strauss, Claude, 59
love, 23, 105
LSD, 79, 91
    as catalyst, 82
    used for personality assessment, 81
    variable pharmacological effects,
        81–82
LSD: My Problem Child (Hofmann), xv,
    33
"LSD and the Cosmic Game" (Grof),
    95
LSD experiences, as religious
    experiences, 21
LSD therapy, 81, 82, 142
    high-dose, 81–83
    low-dose. *See* psycholytic therapy

M

Mahadevan, T. M. P., 69
Mandala IX, 49
Mao Zedong, 136
Maoris, 54

Marx, Karl, 68
Maslow, Abraham, 143
matter, origin of, 66
May, Rollo, 155
meditation, 6, 74n, 104. *See also zazen*
memory, 90. *See also* trauma, reliving
  of birth, 88–89, 92
  gestation/intrauterine, 91, 92, 94
mescaline, 10. *See also* peyote
  effects on brain, 15
  as psychological prism, 10, 11
mescaline experiences, VIII
  compared with mystical
    experience, 20
  Smith's first, 9–13, 46n
metaphysics, 11, 26, 46n
Metzner, Ralph, 10, 46n, 150–51
Mexico, 51
mind, 93, 95. *See also* self
  India's model of, 71
  levels of, 82–83
  modernity's view of, 71–72
  traditional people's view of, 72
  universal, 95–97
mind-body problem, 66–67, 155
Mishlove, Jeffrey, 149–58
morning glories, 49
"mushroom madness," 54
mushrooms, 47n, 49, 51, 51n, 53n, 54,
    151. *See also Amanita muscaria;*
    psilocybin; Soma
  attitudes toward, 54–55
Mushrooms, Russia and History
    (Wasson), 50, 54, 61
musicimol, 57
mysterianism, 67
mystical experience, VIII. *See also*
    religious experiences
mysticism. *See also specific topics*
  types of, 23. *See also* God,
    awareness of
Mysticism, Sacred and Profane
    (Zaehner), 24
Mysticism and Philosophy (Stace),
    21–22, 100

N

N-methyl-D-aspartate (NMDA), 75n
Nagel, Thomas, 67
Native American Church, 31, 113–16,
    119, 123. *See also* Peyote Indians
naturalism, 3
Neconish, Dewey, 118
New Zealand, 54. *See also* aborigines
Newman, John Henry, 107, 108, 111
Nietzsche, Friedrich, 114
nirvana, 72, 92, 131
nitrous oxide, 75
nitrous oxide experiences, IX, XV,
    26–27, 150
Noyes, John Humphrey, 39–40

O

oceanic feeling, 36
O'Flaherty, Wendy Doniger, 49, 53, 58
Oneida Community, 39–40
oneness, vision of, 31
openness and surrender, 138
Ornstein, Robert, 153
Otto, Rudolf, 12

P

Pahnke, Walter, 21, 99, 100, 102–3
pain, 142–43. *See also* suffering
Pain, Sex and Time (Heard), 4–5
pantheonism, 45–50, 46n, 150–51, 153
passion and objectivity, 150
Paul, St., 20
peace and contentment, 28–29, 76, 103
Pentecostal experience, 20
perception, doors of, 74. *See also Doors
    of Perception*
perception-patterning processes, 74n
Perennial Philosophy, The (Huxley), 5, 6
Perfect Being, 4
Peter, St., 19–20
peyote, 18, 116, 119, 130.
    See also mescaline

and bereavement, 125
capacity to change behavior, 123–24
First Amendment and, 113
medicinal and healing qualities,
117–20, 124
moral impact, 120
women, femininity, and, 124–25
Peyote Indians, 23–24, 31, 113. *See also*
Native American Church
phenomenal worlds, 95
philosophy, 5, 6, 21–22
Indian vs. Western, 69–70
Pilat, Albert, 58–59
Pinker, Steven, 67
Plato, ix, 4, 41n, 113, 114
Poisons, Three, 73–75
Polanyi, Michael, 25, 67
polarities, 96–97
pratitya-samutpada, 89–90
prayer, 120–21
Protestantism, 2, 5
psilocybin, 21. *See also* mushrooms
psilocybin experiences, 99–105, 151
psychedelic experience. *See also*
specific topics
inability to integrate it with daily
life, 42
Psychedelic Experience, The (Leary and
Metzner), 150–51, 153
psychedelic movement, conditions
lacking in, 34, 36, 37
antinomianism, 39–41
esoteric/exoteric divide, 41–43
flawed social paradigm, 37–39
Psychedelic Review, 16
psychedelic therapy. *See* LSD therapy,
high-dose
psychoanalysis, 85, 94, 97. *See also*
Freudian model
psycholytic therapy, 81, 83
preliminary/vegetative phase,
83–84, 93
perinatal/Rankian stage, 86, 88, 89,
91, 93

psychodynamic/Freudian stage,
84–85, 88, 89, 91, 93
transpersonal/mystical stage,
86–87, 92, 93
psychosis, 25, 139
purification, 42

Q

qualities, derivation from quantities, 66
quietism, 30, 41

R

raja yoga, 42
Rank, Otto, 86, 94
Rankian stage in psycholytic therapy,
86, 88, 89, 91, 93
Rave, John, 119, 124
reality, ultimate
awareness/sense of, 21, 22
disclosure of, 65
realized self/soul, 76–77
rebirth, 86, 87, 90
regression, 84. *See also* trauma,
reliving; womb
observing ego during, 91
to world of pure perception, 74n
relations, interpersonal, 139
religion(s)
arising from drug-induced
theophanies, 18–19
disillusionment in, 135, 146–47. *See
also* godlessness
drugs and, 17
viewed historically, 18–19
viewed phenomenologically, 19–24
viewed "religiously," 30–32
as escape from reality, 25
new, 146
rationalistic, 30
this-worldly and other-worldly
wings of institutional, 43
religious experiences, 30
as delusions, 31

similarities between drug-induced and non-drug-induced, 19–24, 153
  indistinguishability, 21–23, 26
religious rituals, drugs used in, 18, 80
Renou, Louis, 49, 55
revelations, 22, 63, 141–43. *See also* insights; theophanies
ReVision, 107, 111
Rig-Veda, 47n, 49, 55, 57–59
Riggs, Willie, Sr., 120
Rilke, Rainer Maria, 12
Rioch, Margaret, 141
Roberts, Thomas, 99–105
Rogers, Carl, 155
Russell, Patricia Mousetail, 117–18

S

sacraments, 18, 80
sacred, 141
  sense of the, 75, 78
Sahlins, Marshall, 69
Sargent, Winthrop, 58
satori, 30, 31, 42–43
Satprakashananda, 6
Schneider, Ulrich, 58
Schultes, Richard Evans, 59
science fiction, 146
secret religious knowledge, 41–43, 80
secularization, and the sacred, 135–37, 144, 146–47
Self, 73, 156
self, 73. *See also* ego; mind
  development of sense of, 74n
  normal, 73
  realized, 76–77
  theomorphic view of, 133
  traditional concept of, 72, 79
self-annihilation, 74n, 90. *See also* ego-transcendence
self-centered outlook, 74
self-consciousness, 109n
self-images, 69
separation-individuation, 96

set, 1–4, 20
setting, 4–7, 20
shamanism, 158
Shapiro, Deane, 68–69, 72
Silence, 95
skepticism, irrational, 24–26
sleep, dreamless, 70
Smith, Huston. *See also specific topics*
  experiences with entheogens, 15
  initiation into entheogens, 9–13, 46n
  on Good Friday Experiment, 99–105
  life history, 1–4
  religiosity and religious beliefs, 149–50
  writings, xvi, 45, 46n, 79, 80, 89, 91, 95, 149
Smith, Kendra, 10, 13, 74n
Smith, Wilfred Cantwell, 45
smoking, stopping, 123–24
Snake, Reuben, 113
Soan, Shaku, 76
Soma, 45–52, 53n, 54–56, 60, 62, 80
SOMA (Wasson), 53, 57
  de luxe bookmaking, 61–62
  reviews of, 45, 48, 57–60
soul, 23, 93
  immortality, 47n
  realized, 76–77
Spirit, 93
Stace, Walter T., 21–22, 24, 100
Star Wars, 146
subject/object dichotomy, dissolution of, 36, 87, 92
subtle body, 71, 92
suffering. *See also* pain
  causes of, 87, 90
supernaturalism, 43
Supreme, 95
sura, 56
surgery, painless, 25
surrender and openness, 138
Suzuki, D. T., 41, 144
symbolic expression of unconscious material, 90

T

Tachonie, Irvine, 123
Taittiriya Upanisad, 42
Tantric meditation, 74n
Taoism, 30
telepathy, 157
teonanactl, 50
terminally ill persons, 34, 142
Tertullian, 37–38
theological essays on entheogenic
   drugs, 17
theophanies, 18–19, 34, 80, 141–42.
   See also revelations
  necessary conditions for, 34
  psychedelic, 33–34. *See also* God,
   awareness of
Three Poisons, 72–75
Tillich, Paul, 16, 32
Tipitaka, 41
tragic-flaw theory/device, 72
trance, 156
  painless operations done under
   mesmeric, 25
transcendence, 36, 78, 115, 156–57
trauma
  of birth, 94. *See also* birth process
  reliving, 84
Trauma of Birth, The (Rank), 86, 88

U

UFOs, 132, 146
unconscious
  collective, 154
  individual, 68, 138, 139
  layers of, 74
  physiological, 68
  sacred, 77, 78
  social, 68
unconscious material, symbolic
  expression of, 90
Unger, Sanford, 28

union, mystic, 92
Universal Mind, 95–97
universe
  identification with, 92
  origin of, 65–66
Upanisadic metaphysics, 46n
Upanisads, 42, 49
utopianism, 38

V

values, 154. *See also* evil, rescinded
Varieties of Religious Experience, The
  (James), xv, 150
Varuna, 42
Vedanta, 6, 46, 95
Vedas, 46, 57
Vedic pantheon, gods of the, 45–50,
  46n
vegetative symptoms and phase of
  therapy, 83–84
vinaya, 41
vision quest, 115
visionaries, religious, 25
visions and visual experiences, 6,
  12–13, 23, 84, 110
Void, 95, 130

W

Walsh, Roger, 68–69, 72
Wasson, A. Gordon, viii, xvi, 18, 27,
  45–46, 50–55, 130
"Wasson's SOMA," 45
Watkins, Calvert, 59
Watts, Alan, 131
Wayka, Thomas, 121
Weinberg, Steven, 114
Western models of the mind, 35. *See
  also* Freudian model
White Cloud, Johnny, 124
Whitehead, Alfred North, 46
whole, subsumed by its parts, 87

Wilcox, Ella Wheeler, 132–33
will, 31, 130
Williams, Paris, 119
Wilson, Bill, 129
womb, experience of being in
   regression to, 36
Wordsworth, William, 89
World's Religions, The (Smith), 45, 149
worldviews, VIII
   traditional vs. modern, 69

Y

Yama, 42
yoga, 42, 70

Z

Zaehner, R. C., 20, 23, 24
zazen, 31
Zen Buddhism, 6, 18, 30–31, 40–42, 74, 144

ABOUT THE AUTHOR

Huston Smith, one of the most respected and beloved authorities on world religions, has taught at Washington University, MIT, Syracuse University, and the University of California at Berkeley. Born of missionary parents in Soochow, Smith lived in China until he was seventeen. His youth there provided an appropriate background for his subsequent interest in comparative philosophies and religions. He received his doctorate at the University of Chicago in 1945, and holds twelve honorary degrees. Smith is the father of three daughters. His wife, E. Kendra Smith, Ph.D., is a psychologist.

He is best known for his book *The World's Religions*, which was published in 1958 as *The Religions of Man* and has been translated into twelve languages. It is still one of the most widely used college textbooks on comparative religion, and has sold over two and a half million copies worldwide. Smith believes that the role of what he calls the world's "wisdom traditions" is a simple one: to help us behave decently toward one another. His documentary films on Hinduism, Sufism, and Tibetan Buddhism have all won awards. In 1996, Bill Moyers devoted a five-part PBS special, *The Wisdom of Faith with Huston Smith*, to Smith's life and work.

Sentient Publications, LLC publishes books on cultural creativity, experimental education, transformative spirituality, holistic health, new science, ecology, and other topics, approached from an integral viewpoint. Our authors are intensely interested in exploring the nature of life from fresh perspectives, addressing life's great questions, and fostering the full expression of the human potential. Sentient Publications' books arise from the spirit of inquiry and the richness of the inherent dialogue between writer and reader.

Our Culture Tools series is designed to give social catalyzers and cultural entrepreneurs the essential information, technology, and inspiration to forge a sustainable, creative, and compassionate world.

We are very interested in hearing from our readers. To direct suggestions or comments to us, or to be added to our mailing list, please contact:

SENTIENT PUBLICATIONS, LLC
1113 Spruce Street
Boulder, CO 80302
303-443-2188
contact@sentientpublications.com
www.sentientpublications.com